Stretch Exercises
for Your
HORSE

Stretch Exercises for Your HORSE

The Path to Perfect Suppleness

KARIN BLIGNAULT

TRAFALGAR SQUARE PUBLISHING
NORTH POMFRET, VERMONT

Publisher's Note

The author's previous book, *Successful Schooling – Train Your Horse With Empathy*, to which she makes occasional reference in this text under the abbreviated title *Successful Schooling*, is published by J.A. Allen (London) 1997, ISBN 0.85131.628.X

First published in the United States of America in 2003 by
Trafalgar Square Publishing, North Pomfret, Vermont 05053
Reprinted 2003
Reprinted 2004
Reprinted 2006

Printed in China by Midas Printing International Ltd.

ISBN-10: 1-57076-245-7
ISBN-13: 978-1-57076-245-1
Library of Congress Control Number: 2002115750

Photographs © Alain Proust, except for those on page 23 © *Die Burger*, Capetown,
page 21 © Bob Langrish, pages 19, 61 © Pet Pics, Capetown,
and page 10, by the author.

Line illustrations by Judith Moxon
Design by Judy Linard
Edited by Martin Diggle
Colour separation by Tenon & Polert Colour Scanning Ltd

Contents

Foreword by Claire Waumsley

Many of us talk of writing books over cups of coffee. My friend and colleague Karin Blignault does too – the difference being that she actually writes them.

Stretch Exercises for Your Horse is an important book: an invitation to bring back the old disciplines of the Argentinian Gauchos and Swedish Cavalry Officers, who would not dream of mounting their horse until each muscle and limb had been prodded, pushed, pulled and gentled to perfection; an invitation to develop a ground-level map of your horse with your hands.

Failure to detect early signs of musculoskeletal dysfunction leads inevitably to poor levels of performance and often to more serious injury. Familiarity with your horse's movement range and flexibility within the stretch routines will show up telltale signs of anxiety, fatigue and decreased range of movement long before any serious injury sets in.

In this book, Karin details an extensive routine of exercises with easy-to-use clarity. The depth of information on anatomy and biomechanics will enable the rider to train the horse with increased wisdom, and the veterinarian and physiotherapist will find many helpful ideas to take into account when setting up rehabilitation programmes after injury.

As a physiotherapist, I am delighted that both passive and active stretch exercises have been covered in one book to which I can refer my clients for ongoing maintenance of their horses and for working towards optimal performance levels.

This is not a coffee table book: used properly, it will be found three months after purchase in the tack room, a little discoloured, smelly and nibbled at the corners. Karin, thank you for giving us another tool for bridging the gap of silence between horse and rider.

Claire Waumsley, B.Sc. Physiotherapy (Wits).

Foreword by Freddy Wegelius

Equine sports medicine today needs a lot of tools for maintaining agility and suppleness in the horse during its performance career. What is important for the modern sport horse is a day-to-day routine by which to monitor the biomechanical functions and through which to endeavour to maintain and improve these functions. All horse owners and riders recognize that prevention is inevitably better than cure – yet it is difficult to prevent injuries if the causes of the problem are not properly understood.

Stretch Exercises for Your Horse gives an insight into the way the horse's musculature works and gives us a good hands-on description of how to maintain and improve neuromuscular activity. As Karin Blignault explains, this can be done in an active way by riding the horse and in a passive way by doing the exercises by hand as described. Karin's clear explanation of the procedures to be carried out fosters understanding and thus points the way towards better horse care and management.

From a veterinary point of view one could wish for more scientific exploration and proof of the effects of the stretching exercises. However, from the work that has been done on this issue, the conclusions so far are that stretching exercises maintain and improve gait functionality, soundness of the horse, stride length and suppleness. As a veterinarian who has studied these issues since the mid-1980s, I have found by experience that stretching exercises are of the utmost value as a diagnostic and therapeutic tool in treating musculoskeletal problems in the equine.

Stretch Exercises for Your Horse is a book that emphasizes the value of keeping the equine athlete fit and supple, explains the role and long-term benefits of stretch exercises and, in a pleasant and easy-to-follow way, describes how to put these exercises into practice.

This book will be invaluable for horse owners, riders and all professionals in the equestrian industry whose daily work requires an understanding of the horse's biomechanical properties and muscular functions.

Freddy Wegelius, D.V.M , C.V.A.

Boras, Sweden

About the Author

Karin Blignault was born and raised in Cape Town, South Africa, where she still lives. Always passionately interested in animals, she started riding in her early twenties and studied under a number of eminent trainers – her studies bringing competition success in showjumping, horse trials and dressage. Although a severe knee injury brought a premature end to her participation in jumping competitions, she remains active at a high level in dressage. She also teaches riding, participates in equestrian seminars and enjoys the challenge of correcting problems in other people's horses.

Having studied occupational therapy at Stellenbosch University, Karin took a diploma in the education of children with learning difficulties and then studied neuro-developmental therapy at the Bobath Centre in London. Following this, she went on to lecture on the development of visual perception and learning theory at Cape Town University.

As her studies and career progressed, Karin became increasingly aware of the parallels between communication techniques and the facilitation of movement in disabled children, and the key concepts of classical equitation. Further exploration of these parallels, in which she combined her knowledge of anatomy and neurology with her equestrian expertise, led to her writing the highly acclaimed *Successful Schooling – Train Your Horse with Empathy*. Now, further combining her skills with the latest specialist research, she has produced *Stretch Exercises for Your Horse*, a book which shows how techniques, long considered invaluable in the field of human athletics and gymnastics, can be applied with great benefit to that equine athlete and gymnast – the modern sport horse.

Acknowledgements

Once again I give thanks and all the credit to the Almighty who has guided my life so that all the pieces of the puzzle of life are slowly fitting together to make perfect sense. Without the strength and guidance I get from Him, I am nothing.

To my long-time friend, Judith Moxon, who patiently drew and redrew the illustrations so perfectly, thank you. Not only for the illustrations, but also for being a pillar of strength and support for me.

I owe a great debt to Alain Proust, an outstanding professional photographer, who kindly offered his assistance one morning and ended up taking the bulk of the photographs. I am most grateful for all his time, patience and considerable expertise in taking these beautiful photographs. It is hard to believe that this was his first equine photo shoot.

How can I possibly thank Claire Waumsley enough? She is probably one of the best physiotherapists around, broadminded and knowledgeable – a walking encyclopaedia indeed. She managed to find answers to all of my queries. Claire, this book is yours as much as it is mine. Eva Kjellsdotter, together with Claire, taught me most of the passive stretch exercises. My thanks and appreciation go to both of them.

To Dr Freddy Wegelius, the eminent veterinary surgeon from Sweden, who provided the results of research done under his guidance and gave of his knowledge so freely and selflessly, my heartfelt thanks. I would also like to thank Dr du Plessis ('Dr Dup') who answered my veterinary questions with such generosity.

To Caroline Burt, my publisher, who is always so positive, encouraging and supportive, thanks for making me feel that my work is special. I also thank my editor, Martin Diggle, who painstakingly removed the gremlins from this work, and Judy Linard for her expert design work. A special word of thanks to my son Nico, who spent many hours drawing the diagrams on a computor not designed for the job.

Lastly, I thank André Blignault who, many years ago, suggested that I write a book on Yoga for Horses!

Glossary

This glossary provides a brief explanation of various terms used within the main text. Where a description includes another term in this glossary, that term is set in italic.

Adbuction The movement of a limb sideways, or partially sideways, away from the body.

Adduction The movement of a limb sideways, or partially sideways, towards the body.

Agonists The muscles which actively produce movement by contracting. (As a consequence, they are also referred to as movers.)

Antagonists Those muscles which oppose the *agonists*. (The antagonists have to relax to enable the agonists to contract.)

Automatic reactions Reactions of the body over which the mind does not have voluntary control. These include the automatic effect of gravity upon the muscles, automatic *balance reactions* and automatic *righting reactions*.

Balance reaction The *automatic reaction* of the body which enables it to maintain balance by adjusting its weight distribution and rearranging its posture when balance it disturbed. (For example, when any person loses balance, they will automatically raise their arms to adjust weight distribution in an attempt to avoid falling over.)

Biomechanics The mechanical principles by which a living body functions.

Concentric contraction Normal muscular contraction during which the muscles are shortened to close the angle of a joint.

Coloidial gel The jelly-like material of the *fascia* within which the fibres of the fascia lie.

Dislocation When the articular surfaces of a joint are completely dissociated from each other. (See also *subluxation*.)

Dorsal The back of the body and limbs.

Eccentric contraction A gradual release of muscular contraction against an external force, such as gravity. The muscle contracts while it returns to its relaxed length. For example, when lowering the arm from a horizontal position, the deltoid muscle on the shoulder contracts eccentrically while it is lengthening. It is important to note that a muscle can be in a full state of contraction without shortening and that this state is possible at any length of its range.

End range (or outer and inner range) **of movement** Refers to the widest as well as the smallest angle in which a joint can move, that is, full extension and full flexion. (See also *range of movement*.)

Extension In physiological terms, straightening of the body and limbs (see also *flexion*.)

Fascia A packing medium for bones, muscles and vessels of the body.

Flexion (See also *extension*.) Bending of the body and limbs. The term flexion is also used to describe a yielding of the horse's poll and jaw to the rider's aids and, more generally, a rounding of the horse's body in the longitudinal plane.

Joint capsule The cuff of soft tissue surrounding a joint. It contains the joint fluid (synovial fluid) and thus allows smooth movement of the joint. If the joint capsule becomes inflamed, extra fluid is secreted into the joint space, producing swelling.

Kinesthetic sense The automatic awareness of the position and movement of the different parts of the body at all times.

Mid-range of movement The most comfortable range in which a joint moves: it reaches neither full extension nor full flexion. When a joint operates only in mid-range, the total range of movement will slowly diminish. (See also *range of movement*.)

Muscle tone Refers to the degree of tension in the muscles, even at rest. Each animal has a unique basic muscle tone, which may range from low to high. Very supple horses usually have low muscle tone – their movement is thus free and 'loose' – whereas horses with high muscle tone usually have short, 'choppy' movement. Muscle tone is increased through exercise, tension and anxiety.

Neuro-muscular principles The physiological principles by which the nerves control the muscles.

Nuchal apparatus The ligamentous apparatus which runs from the horse's poll, over the back, to the tail. The front part consists of the strong nuchal ligament, which is attached to the cervical spine by the nuchal fascia. This allows free movement of the head and neck. Further back, spanning the thoracic and lumbar regions, is the supraspinous ligament. This has a different consistency from the nuchal ligament, its purpose being to stabilize the vertebrae and prevent unwanted movement.

Patella The small bone which is embedded in the tendon of the quadriceps femoris muscle of the hind leg. Together, these components comprise what is referred to as the stifle joint.

Periosteum The tough, fibrous membrane surrounding bone.

Phasic muscles Those muscles which are responsible for skeletal movement.

Proprioception The information which arises from the body, especially from the muscles, joints, ligaments and receptors associated with bones. The *kinesthetic* sense is dependent on this information.

Protraction Movement away from the body in a forward-backward plane.

Range of movement The extent to which a joint can move. Passive movement range is usually greater than active movement range. Tight muscles, tendons and ligaments usually restrict the range of movement. (See also *end range* and *mid-range of movement*.)

Reciprocal apparatus The specific pattern of muscle and tendon connections in the horse's hind leg which leads to the stifle and hock joints always extending or flexing simultaneously.

Reflex-response time The time taken from the moment of stimulation to the moment of response.

Retraction Movement backwards towards the body in a forward-backward plane.

Righting reaction The automatic reactions to align the head, trunk and limbs correctly with the earth's surface, so that the animal can move away from danger with greater ease.

Sesamoiditis Inflammation of the sesamoid bone, usually caused by the tight tendon attachment on this bone.

Startle reflex The automatic reaction of an animal to sudden noises, sudden movements or strange objects. Heartbeat, blood pressure and adrenalin levels all rise and the animal takes on an alert stance, ready to flee.

Subluxation When the articular surfaces of a joint are partly dissociated from each other, but partial contact remains. (See also *dislocation*.)

Synergists A group of muscles which all work together to produce a specific movement.

Therapeutic technique A treatment technique which enhances functional healing.

Tonic muscles Those muscles which are responsible for the maintenance of postural control, balance and stability.

Ventral The front of the body or limbs.

Viscoelasticity The liquid in soft tissue is thick and sticky when cold. When it is warmed or shaken (as during exercise), it becomes more liquid (less viscous), and its flow is improved. When the body is standing still, the liquid cools and reverts back to its thick, sticky state. Warming thus releases the muscle stiffness caused by the viscosity of the cold liquid. The high viscosity of resting muscle allows maintenance of a given posture without unnecessary expenditure of energy. The fluidity of this liquid combined with the capacity of the muscles to stretch determines the degree of muscular suppleness.

Introduction

The stretching of muscles has been an integral part of the training of the human athlete for many years. At each gymnastic or athletic performance we see athletes and gymnasts doing their warming up together with their stretching exercises as a preventative measure against injury. Recent research has shown that active stretching should be done both before exercise to help tone the muscles and ensure a good range of movement, and after exercise to lengthen the muscles to the same state they were in before commencing the exercise. A Swedish study showed that strength training without stretching at the conclusion of the exercise led to the range of movement being restricted for 2–3 days. When the muscles were stretched after strength training, the movement range remained normal.[1] Yet we see little stretching in the warm-up of the equine athlete, be it racing, jumping or dressage.

Many riders experience discomfort resulting from shortened tendons and muscles in their own bodies. These are usually the leg adductors – the riding muscles – and the shortening is demonstrated practically by an inability to do the 'splits'. The excessive and repeated contraction and strengthening of these muscles during riding will eventually shorten them unless they are put through a daily stretch programme. Should the rider wish to render these muscles more flexible again, it will be necessary to do regular stretching exercises. Another group of muscles commonly shortened is the hamstring muscles, which prevent us from touching our toes while keeping the knees straight. These muscles and tendons can all be stretched by repetition and if we work at it diligently we will finally be able to touch our toes or do the 'splits' and be more comfortable in

[1] Möller, M., Oeberg, B., Ekstrand, J. and Gillquist, J., The Effect of a Strength Training Programme on Flexibility (Art.), Swedish Society of Sports Medicine 1981.

Figure 1. Human athletic stretch exercises. The stretching of muscles, together with muscle strengthening exercises, endurance training and speed and co-ordination exercises, have become integral elements of the fitness training of all athletes. Each of these factors influences the total performance of the athlete. Suppleness is important not only for the achievement of maximum athletic ability, but also to minimize the chances of muscle, tendon and ligament injuries. That is why all track and field athletes, swimmers and gymnasts stretch both actively and passively. Some local gymnasia even offer stretching classes for amateurs. The athletes pictured here are stretching respectively (a) the calf muscles and (b) the quadriceps femoris muscle.

(a)   (b)

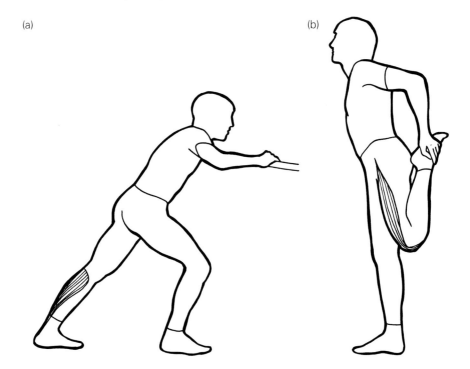

general. As a consequence of stretching the horse's muscles he, too, should become more supple and comfortable. Although there are intrinsic metabolic differences in the muscular activity of humans and horses, the basic neuro-muscular principles are identical. Therefore the reasons for stretching muscles are identical in both species.

One of the major objectives in the training of horses for athletic or gymnastic performance is to keep them free from injury while reaching for maximum performance – be it maximum stride length, perfect jumping ability or greater speed in racing. Muscle strain injuries, of one form or another, are often the cause of inadequate performance in sport horses. This book will show how these injuries can be prevented through a stretch programme.

Many veterinarians and physiotherapists are strong supporters of stretch exercises for horses as a precaution to prevent injuries. A few such authorities are:

Dr Freddy Wegelius[2] from Sweden who, with two students, has done intensive studies of stretch exercises for horses. They were able to prove that passive stretch exercises improve passive range of movement in the horse significantly. Dr Wegelius has developed a basic passive muscle stretch programme in consultation with equine therapist Matti Kautto.[3]

Dr James Waldsmith, a veterinarian attached to the Equine Centre in California, who states: 'The single most important therapeutic technique a rider can learn, in order to prevent injury, is to do passive stretching exercises with his horse'.

Dr Hilary M. Clayton from Michigan State University, who wrote a chapter on stretching/suppling exercises in her book *Conditioning Sport Horses*.

Sarah Wyche MRCVS, who wrote: 'It may seem like wizardry when we have watched a horse struggle to perform a certain movement and suddenly find he is able to move freely. Rest assured, however, not even the professional equine therapists use magic wands. What they do is stretch! They may actually stretch part of a limb or muscle, or they may cause a muscle or ligament to stretch as part of a reflex response. Nevertheless, by stretching, and thereby redeeming the correct balance of tension across the horse's muscles and joints, the energy flows and the mobility returns'.[4]

---

[2] Wegelius, Dr F, How to Maintain and Improve Athletic Performance in the Horse by Means of Passive Stretching Exercises (Lecture).
[3] Kauto, M., Stretching of The Horse (Poster), Alingsås, Sweden.
[4] Wyche, S.,'The Balance of Change. Tissue Transformations – As if by Magic? (Art.) *Dressage* August 2000.

Although it is not based on scientifically reliable statistical testing, there is some evidence that dressage horses, through active lateral stretching, are more supple laterally than showjumpers. Showjumpers, however, have more flexibility in stretching their forelegs forwards, than do ordinary riding horses.

Although many of the exercises described in this book are used by physiotherapists, they are not to be considered solely for therapeutic use. They are available for lay people to use to improve their horses' abilities and they are a means of maintaining the horse in optimum condition by doing both active suppling exercises under saddle and passive suppling exercises off the horse. Once suppleness has been developed, it has to be maintained by incorporating regular suppling exercises in the horse's workout programme.

Not all ridden horses are perfect for the job at hand. Some horses – for example, some Arabians – have beautiful, eye-catching, free-flowing movement, but the wrong conformation for the collection required in Grand Prix dressage. Examples of such conformation include a high croup, straight hind legs or too low a neck carriage. Regular stretching can help a croup-high, straight-legged horse to engage his hind legs. Other horses have a perfect temperament, but inadequate movement. Yet others combine power with tractability, but do not have enough lateral suppleness. This does not apply only to potential dressage horses – for example, straightening a racehorse may give him the opportunity to win races (see page 22).

Very few of us are lucky enough to possess the perfect horse. Many riders pass on horses who are less than perfect until they find the horse with all the necessary attributes for their specific purpose. This often takes years and can be very expensive – and large amounts of time and money are luxuries which many riders do not possess. While professional riders are constantly in search of the ultimate horse, they usually have a string of horses at different training levels. Thus, if one of whom they had high hopes does not make the grade, at least they do not have to start a new horse from scratch. It can take a long time to ascertain that your horse cannot do a brilliant passage and to start over again will waste many valuable years. Most riders, however, purchase a horse to keep forever. They find that the bond they build is far too painful to break just for the sake of that elusive quality, perfection. In many cases, a rider may establish a great relationship with a particular horse, who is highly suitable in many aspects, but does not have the correct movement to compete successfully in a specific discipline. Stretching exercises could make the difference in many cases, and may be a welcome alternative to purchasing a new horse.

In the following pages I will not only endeavour to convince you that a programme of stretch exercises is essential for most equine athletes, but also to motivate you to start your own stretch programme for your horse. This book is conveniently bound to be taken to the stable so that you can try the exercises on your horse.

NOTE

During active stretch exercises the horse stretches more than one synergistic group of muscles. That is to say, an exercise which primarily targets a specific group of muscles will also activate other muscles that work together with that group. This interaction is heightened by the fact that the whole body also functions as a unit as a consequence of the various automatic reactions, and thus bending one area will necessitate bending in another area. When the neck flexes it influences the whole horse down the spine because of the body's righting reaction and the fact that the spine works as a unit. Therefore, many of the mounted exercises are repeated in the stretching of the different areas of the horse's body. The rider will soon find that doing one exercise, such as shoulder-in, will have an effect on the stretching ability of the neck, trunk, forelegs and, to some extent, the hind legs. Notwithstanding the fact that the body functions as a unit, for the purposes of this book, the horse's body has been divided into different sections. This 'division' of the horse will help the reader to visualize the area to stretch for a particular purpose. While presenting the material in this way has necessitated the repetition of the active stretch exercises, I feel that this will be more helpful to the reader than constantly referring back to previous pages, especially since the book is intended for use in a practical context.

While detailed instructions are given for all the passive stretch exercises mentioned, I would stress that the purpose of this book is not to describe the active (mounted) stretch exercises in detail, or to teach how the horse should be trained to do them. Detailed instructions on teaching the horse these movements can be found in my book *Successful Schooling – Train Your Horse with Empathy*.

CHAPTER 1

The Importance of Stretching

The objects of muscle stretching are to improve performance by maintaining or regaining optimum mobility and suppleness, and to reduce injury by reducing the tension on joints, tendons, muscles and ligaments.

Preventing Muscle Injury

Competition horses are athletes and, as such, they need to have their maximum potential developed. When training horses for athletic or gymnastic performance it is essential to keep them free from injury. Unfortunately, the rigorous training they go through to reach the top often causes muscle and tendon injuries. Maintaining suppleness in a competition horse is an important element in preventing strain injuries. Doing passive, as well as active, stretch exercises will maintain suppleness in the horse. The muscular problems experienced by horses in competition have many similarities to those experienced by their human counterparts. These problems are caused by the strain and exertion required in pushing the athlete to ever greater levels of achievement.

Knowing when to stop pushing for that bigger lateral step or longer stride in trot is the secret to injury prevention. Push too hard and you will cause injury to the muscles, tendons or ligaments. The human athlete can feel when he is pushing too hard and cease the exercise when appropriate, but his equine counterpart has no definitive language in which to tell the rider/trainer that the strain is too much. The rider/trainer may not be perceptive enough to pick up the distress signals and by the time realization dawns that the horse is taking strain, it is often too late to prevent damage. The old adage 'prevention is better than cure', becomes especially relevant in the training of the equine athlete because the recovery period can be very long and expensive. Correct stretching of muscles is a way of preventing many strain and ligament sprain injuries.

Muscles are stretched to maintain or regain full length of the muscle fibres. By being longer they are automatically more supple. By being more supple and pre-stretched the muscles and tendons are less prone to stretch injuries. Tendons are not very elastic; they are dependent on the elasticity of the body of the muscle itself.

The muscle and tendon together cover a precise space between origin and attachment. When the muscle is shortened and inflexible, the tendon is constantly on stretch. When the muscle is longer and supple, the tendon does not pull on the bone and cause inflammation, or strain the joint.

Tight, shortened muscles are thus usually the cause of tendon injuries, which are possibly the most common soft tissue injury in the sport horse.[1] When the muscles are tight the tendons can tear when the associated muscle is put under stress because of overstretch. Stretch injuries can occur during sudden strong exertions such as in showjumping or jumping out of the starting stalls in racing, or simply when playing in the paddock. Muscle strain injuries or torn muscles are usually caused by a sudden stretch that takes the muscle beyond its physiological limit. Injury can also occur from the overuse of extended gaits, which puts undue strain on the ligaments and tendons (for example, the suspensory ligament when gallop-ing and the check ligament when maintaining the extended trot). Riding for long periods at extended trot, as some endurance riders tend to do, puts the limbs in full stretch. This leaves little margin for error. Loss of co-ordination in any form (a slip, stumbling on rough terrain, or fatigue) can overstrain or tear a ligament or tendon.

Since stretching reduces muscular tension, it thereby helps to prevent muscle strain. Stretching also improves the elasticity and flexibility of the muscles, tendons and ligaments, reducing the chances of their being overstretched. Thus a supple horse is less likely to injure himself as his muscles and tendons are better prepared to adapt to sudden changes of direction, speed and terrain and to the occasionally over-zealous requests of the rider or trainer.

[1] Snow, Dr D.H., Vogel, Dr C.J., *Equine Fitness. The Care and Training of the Athletic Horse*, Trafalgar Square Farm Book, David and Charles, Inc. (North Pomfret) 1987, p59.

Muscle fatigue is another common cause of injury to joints, ligaments, muscles and tendons. The strain on the tendon is greater when the muscle to which it is attached becomes fatigued. This leads to diminished co-ordination of movement, which can then cause the injury. Tight and shortened muscles will fatigue more rapidly than supple muscles.

Ligaments are the bands of tough, fibrous tissue connecting bones at a joint.

Figure 2. Ligaments of the hock: (a) lateral view, (b) medial view.

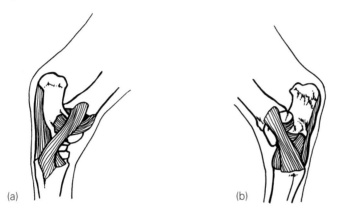

(a)   (b)

Ligaments, tendons, and the joint capsules secure and stabilize the joints, and define their range of movement. They prevent subluxations (partial dislocations) and actual dislocations of the joint. A joint without these soft tissue attachments would be capable of a substantial but unregulated range of movement. In fact, joints protected by hyper-flexible ligaments have abnormally large ranges of movement, as acrobatic performers and contortionists in the circus demonstrate clearly. However, we are not aiming for these abnormal ranges of movement in the horse, but simply for optimal movement. To ensure the optimal range of movement, the muscles, tendons and ligaments have to be supple. Stretching, which optimizes the range of movement in the joints, will reduce the incidence of injuries. For example, the relatively acute angle of impact when the foot hits the ground during a longer stride, and the length of time it then stays on the ground, provide more shock absorption than is afforded by the more perpendicular angle of the short stride.

Thus stretching helps to prevent ligament sprain and helps to keep the joint capsules flexible. Overstretching of the joint capsule and ligaments, however, will lead to instability of the joints. These should only be mobilized under veterinary supervision. Protecting the ligaments is of *fundamental* importance in the sport horse. The most severe form of strain injury to a horse is ligament injury. It has repercussions beyond the damage to the ligament itself and the tissue takes a year to regain only 90 per cent of its former strength.

The bowed tendon on the near fore is the result of a racing injury.

Another form of stress injury can be caused by maintaining a fixed position for a long period. Examples of this include maintaining a fixed neck position (whether or not this entails holding the neck down with running reins) and training with no rest periods. Continuous work in a small range of movement and endless, repetitive exercises are extensions of such work and lead to a form of stress injury which, in humans, is called RSI (repetitive strain injury) or occupational overuse syndrome and is a major cause of long-term disability.

In order to prevent such problems in the horse, regular stretch periods in a long frame and working in the outer ranges of movement should be alternated with the fixed isometric muscle contractions (working muscles at a fixed length-loading) which occur during dressage training in small movement ranges (collection). The ability to contract the muscles in the outer ranges of movement is of importance for horses if they are to reach the top of their discipline. Perhaps this is one of the reasons why some very talented horses never fulfil their potential. Muscles work most easily and efficiently in their middle range of movement. Working at either the inner (shortened) or outer (elongated) ranges of movement is more difficult and requires a higher degree of suppleness and strength.

When a horse is doing active stretching, the muscles work while they are stretching and this produces supple, but strong, muscles through improving the quality of the muscle fibres. For gymnastic purposes muscles need to be supple as well as strong. Strength without suppleness can lead to injuries during those exercises that need supple muscles, such as half-passes and jumping (which requires a supple back). Similarly, suppleness without strength can lead to injuries during exercises that need power and stability, such as jumping (which, in this context, places demands on the hamstrings) and the canter pirouette.

Muscle imbalance is a significant cause of injury and myofascial (muscle tissue) pain in the sport horse. Muscle imbalance develops when mobility and suppleness are not maintained in exercise or when there is inadequate exercise, or inactivity. This can lead to muscle overload and injury. The tonic muscles, which are responsible for postural control, stability and balance, then become shortened, while the phasic muscles, which produce movement, become weakened. This imbalance creates a vicious circle. Too much concentration on strength exercises of the tonic (postural) muscles, with the resultant shortening, will lead to weakness of the phasic (movement) muscles. The weakening of the phasic muscles then leads to further shortening of the tonic muscles. The shortened tonic muscles are generally more active than the weakened phasic muscles, as they produce defensive and protective movements such as those of the back extensors and the adductors of the front and rear limbs. (The adductors are those muscles that act to move the limb towards the horse's body.) This leads to mechanical overloading and muscle strains or tears in the shortened muscles. These shortened muscles are more prone to strain injury as they are less elastic and supple in the relaxation phase. The particular equine muscles that show a tendency to shorten are the pectorals and biceps brachii in the front limb, the adductors, the iliopsoas and the hamstrings in the hind limb, and the back extensors. The muscles that tend to weaken are the triceps muscle in the forelimb, the gluteals and quadriceps femoris in the hind limb, and the abdominal muscles.

This imbalance can cause problems of co-ordination, as when the gluteal muscles have to relax to plant the hind leg (see pages 17–18). Muscle imbalance also puts more strain on the joints, causing inflammation. Overloading of the weakened muscles will also lead to myofascial (muscle tissue) pain.

A programme of stretch exercises for the tonic muscles and strengthening for the phasic muscles can prevent as well as remedy this particular problem of muscular imbalance. Stretching and suppling exercises have to precede strengthening. The weak muscles can only strengthen once the tonic muscles have lengthened. *Active* stretch exercises, to some extent, incorporate strengthening of the antagonists (the muscle 'pairs' which produce the opposite movement to those being stretched) and are thus the ideal method of starting the stretch programme. 'If the imbalance is allowed to continue, the muscular susceptibility to injury will increase'.[2]

Upward fixation of the patella (locking stifle) is a fairly common condition in horses and is caused by muscle imbalance. The limb becomes locked in extension because the medial plantar ligament locks over the medial trochlea and the femur. This is usually a consequence of muscle wastage after a debilitating disease, the horse being in poor condition, of poor muscular development, or of incorrect conformation in young horses. Stretching the medial ligament of the stifle in a passive adductor stretch, active stretching in lateral work, together with improving the condition and strengthening of the muscles should alleviate this condition.

Alleviating and Preventing Pain

Stretch exercise relieves pain caused by muscle spasm and injury and helps to prevent muscle spasms. Passive stretching after exercise can help to reduce myofascial pain – often referred to as trigger points. Trigger points are small, tender points in a muscle. When palpated, these circumscribed points can be felt as nodules or hard bands in the muscle. The nodules are thought to be small contractures (shrinkages) of muscle fibres

[2] Spring, H., Illi, U., Kunz, H., Röthlin, K., Schneider, W. and Tritschler, T., *Stretching and Strengthening Exercises*, Thieme Medical Publishers, Inc. (New York) 1991, p5.

in specific areas of a muscle and to have restricted blood circulation, with resultant oxygen starvation. This, in turn, leads to the build-up of waste products of metabolism in the muscle. When compressed, the nodules are exquisitely painful and can trigger referred pain, which is felt at a distance, often completely remote from its source. That is why pain over a joint area may be secondary to a trigger point in a muscle and can be incorrectly diagnosed as a joint inflammation. If the painful trigger point is treated with pressure or acupuncture, the 'joint' pain will disappear altogether. If the primary trigger point is not dealt with, it can lead to trigger points in both synergists and antagonists and to pain-induced muscle spasm. These factors, in turn, cause pain to be referred to still more distant sites. Over the course of time, the pain may spread to affect a large, ever-increasing area. If untreated, this can become a long-term problem.

Trigger points become activated through pain-induced muscle spasm, when the muscle fibres stay contracted because of direct trauma to the muscle, acute overload, overstretch and overwork fatigue (repetitive, sustained contractions without sufficient rest periods). Tight muscles which lack suppleness exacerbate these trigger points. Muscles containing active trigger points become shorter and weaker. Any attempt to extend the muscle actively will result in pain. Trigger points are treated by a physiotherapist with deep pressure and acupuncture. However, as stated, keeping the muscles supple with sufficient active and passive stretch exercises can prevent them from forming.

Stretching also helps to reduce friction between the different soft tissues. By maintaining suppleness, the different soft tissues are assisted to glide through each other – for example, nerves and blood vessels glide through muscles and ligaments.

Improving Performance

Stretch exercises improve performance through the improvement of different biomechanical functions such as range of movement, co-ordination and balance.

Range of Movement

Each horse has both an active and a passive range of movement. The active range of movement is the extent to which a limb will move by the horse's own voluntary effort. The passive range of movement is the extent to which a limb can move when the movement is produced by an outside force, in the context of this book, the handler. Increased elasticity, flexibility and suppleness of the muscles, tendons and ligaments will increase the horse's passive range of movement through greater joint mobility. A larger active range of movement produces more power in the stride as well as more momentum because the hind legs push against the ground with more force when they linger on it for a longer period of time.

In addition to each horse having his own particular range of movement, each joint also has a specific range of movement, which is different in each individual horse. Therefore, no two horses move in exactly the same manner. As competitive riders we would like our horses to use their maximum range to achieve maximum performance. To ensure that this range of movement, once achieved, is not lost, each joint has to move through its full range at least once a day. This has an added benefit in that it will show you when the horse is taking strain. The older the horse, the stiffer he becomes if he is not stretched or suppled up daily. Besides age, other causes of losing range are previous injury, repeated strains and exertions and the over-development of muscles. Strong muscles are often shortened muscles. Short, tight muscles put more stress on their areas of origin and attachment – the tendons on the bone. This will lead to inflammatory conditions such as sesamoiditis. That is why treating the joint alone will not lead to a permanent solution. Power exercises increase the size and strength of the muscles. As a muscle becomes stronger, physical resistance becomes stronger because the balance between the agonist and antagonist (the muscle and its opposing 'pair' – see Figure 3 and Chapter 2, page 34) becomes tighter and the range of movement shortens. When the agonist contracts, the antagonist, which is now strong, short and tight, will give more resistance to the contraction of the agonist. To reduce this resistance suppleness, achieved through stretching, is required. The training programme should first aim at freedom of movement (suppleness) and, only after this has been developed, should power and strength in the collected gaits be improved.

Through stretching exercises the tension and resistance in the muscles, tendons and ligaments are reduced, thereby improving and maintaining the range of joint movement. Joint range should, however not be increased beyond the horse's normal range, as this will cause instability. The horse should not have hyper-mobile joints.

Strength, together with suppleness (reduction of resistance) will enhance performance, whether in the form of a longer stride in racing, generally bigger movement in dressage, or a bigger jump. This is because the muscles are made longer and more flexible, the joints become more flexible and this leads to freer movement and bigger gaits. Of course, this does not mean that a poor mover can be stretched to become an outstanding mover. Such work will, however, definitely improve his movement and allow the horse to move at his own optimum level.

Figure 3. Diagrams to illustrate agonist contraction with antagonist relaxation in the human and the horse.

(a) The biceps muscle (agonist) contracts while the triceps muscle (antagonist) relaxes and stretches.

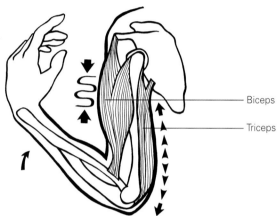

Biceps

Triceps

(b) The brachiocephalic muscle (agonist) contracts while the latissimus dorsi and teres major (antagonists) relax and stretch.

(c) The latissimus dorsi and teres major (in this case, the agonists) contract while the brachiocephalic muscle stretches.

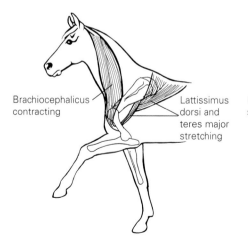

Brachiocephalicus contracting

Lattissimus dorsi and teres major stretching

Brachiocephalicus stretching

Lattissimus dorsi and teres major contracting

15

Remedial stretching to enhance range of movement

A horse is often left with a diminished range of movement after injury, when the trauma to the soft tissue has healed. This may be a result of adhesions, or simply joint stiffness arising from stable rest. Remedial stretching helps to break up scar tissue and re-align the tissues to reduce contracture. It loosens adhesions in the muscle fibres, which leads to more flexibility, and it mobilizes the joints and so increases the range of movement. Remedial stretching should be done under professional supervision.

Co-ordination and Balance

The following three concepts will help with the understanding of how balance is maintained.

Proprioception. This sense allows the brain to perceive all movement, vibrations, stretch, or anything that affects the muscles, tendons and joints, as well as informing the brain of all changes of movement. It allows the brain to know exactly what every muscle is doing at any given moment, independent of the sense of sight. Thus the disturbance of balance is perceived instantly by the proprioceptive sensory organs, which are situated in the joints, tendons and muscle ends. It is through this sense of proprioception that the horse will clear an obstacle with his forelegs and also, without seeing them, clear it with his hind legs.

Body awareness. This is the knowledge of where every part of the body is at all times and it is dependent on the proprioceptive sense.

Body Schema. In order to maintain balance the muscles have to adapt continuously to compensate for movement in another area. For example, should you raise one arm there will be an instant and automatic adaptation in another part of the body to keep the body arranged, in perfect balance, around the centre of gravity. The body schema is always changing to adapt to movement; it is an automatic process designed to ensure that an animal retains balance. External factors such as a very heavy, unbalanced rider on a little horse may compromise its efficiency.

Good co-ordination and balance improve the quality of movement. A number of complementary factors contribute to this. If improvements are made to elasticity, flexibility, range of movement and reflex response time, then the reaction speed of movement is increased. The horse thus becomes more co-ordinated. Stretching, which contributes to these improvements, also improves the circulation of blood and lymphatic fluids. This increased circulation allows for more oxygen and nutrients to reach and replenish the muscles and for toxic by-products of metabolism to be removed more efficiently, thus improving the recovery time in the contraction-relaxation sequence and preventing fatigue. This improved circulation thus improves the reflex response time. Every muscle goes through a phase of contraction and a phase of relaxation. After each contraction the muscle has to relax and recoup for the next contraction. Athletic ability is not only dependent on the ability of the muscles to contract, but also on the speed with which the opposing muscle (the antagonist) can relax. The quicker the opposing muscle can relax, the faster the agonist can contract. The more the relaxation, the stronger the contraction. Therefore, the faster the muscles can relax, the better the horse's performance will be, whether in terms of speed, jumping or dressage movements. Through stretching, the reflex time is decreased, thus the antagonists relax quicker.

The improvement that stretching makes to range of movement also enhances body awareness through improved proprioception. This in turn leads to improved balance. At the ends of the muscles there are cells known as Golgi cells (see The Golgi Apparatus in Chapter 2). These cells are incredibly sensitive to changes in the muscles and they relate to the brain (central nervous system) what is happening in the muscle. A tug on the Golgi cells will automatically stimulate them. Stretching thus improves body awareness and body schema, which in turn leads to improved balance and co-ordination. It is also the case that a supple horse has more control over his balance. Not only is he less likely to move out of his balance but, since his reflex responce is faster, he can restore any loss of balance faster.

Remedial stretching to enhance co-ordination and balance

Muscles store a memory of pain ('muscle memory') and will shorten to avoid pain and become tense.[3] This shortening will lead to diminished co-ordination. According to Berna Lindfield, a horse may shorten his range of movement to guard against pain in his gluteal muscles. This reaction is exacerbated by the fact that, because of the pain, the muscles cannot relax. 'The gluteals contract to push the horse over his

[3] Rossi, E. L., and Check, D., *Mind-Body Therapy (Psycho-biology of Injury and Physiological Tissue Memory)*, W. Norton & Co. (USA) 1994.

planted hind leg. At the moment the other hind leg has to plant, the gluteals of the leg in stance have to stop contracting (do nothing). If this does not happen because of "perceived pain" or "adaptive muscle shortening", the stride will shorten and become uneven.'[4] When the actual pain is removed, the horse will still be left with the shortened muscles which will continue to affect the co-ordination. Only through a stretch programme will the co-ordination become normal again.

Jumping Ability

Stretching improves jumping ability by allowing more flexibility in the back and neck muscles. During the jump the horse has to stretch his neck in order to bascule. This bascule helps the horse to jump higher. Through the stretch in the back – and especially the neck – the horse is able to improve his bascule. This is because the horse uses his head and neck as a bob weight to move his centre of gravity forwards and backwards, and the neck therefore has a major effect on the horse's balance and ability to jump. Longitudinal and lateral suppleness in the horse's neck are therefore essential in order to develop the horse's jumping ability.

Suppleness elsewhere is also important. Supple leg muscles allow the horse to curl up his forelegs more and to bring his hind legs further up underneath his abdomen. Suppleness in the shoulders improves the ability to lift the forelimbs. Supple lumbo-sacral and hip joints improve his ability to lift the hindquarters out of the way of the obstacle. The muscles responsible for extension of the hip and stifle can only stretch when the opposing group of muscles contract. These contracting muscles enhance strength and power in jumping. During the landing phase of jumping, one fetlock will be subjected to a force of over 3 tons (2722 kg) of weight. Imagine the stretch the horse will need in his digital and carpal flexor muscles to absorb this weight. Tendons have remarkable tensile strength, and supple forearm muscles enhance this strength by allowing more flexibility in the fetlocks. If the muscle cannot stretch, the tendon cannot absorb this weight. There are no muscles below the horse's knee or hock, only the long tendons. The muscles which allow the feet to function are all situated above the knee (in the forearm) and above the hock. Stiff fetlocks pull on the muscles. When these muscles are not supple the tendons will take strain. According to Dr Wegelius, flexible fetlocks are strong fetlocks. He would rather see fetlocks with grazes from stretching onto the ground than those with restricted movement.

[4] Lindfield, B., (Art.), C.H.A.P. Newsletter Spring 2000. (Notes by Heather Hodge).

Photographs of the horse's legs folding up during a jump.

(a) Note the stretch of the triceps muscle and contraction of the biceps muscle in the opposing muscle group of the foreleg.

(b) Note the stretch of the quadriceps femoris and tensor fascia lata in the hind limb.

Both jumping and dressage horses frequently strain their lumbar and gluteal muscles. A stretch programme can prevent such strain.

Dressage Performance

Stretch exercises enhance the classical training of a horse. Although following a classical training programme will usually lead to a supple and straight horse, some horses can be naturally less supple in one area and more supple in another. For instance, some dressage horses may have more suppleness in their forelimbs than in their hind limbs. Others may be more supple laterally than longitudinally. Horses who have more suppleness in their hind leg extensors (gluteal muscles) than in their hind leg adductors, can engage more readily than they can do half-passes. In such cases, putting more emphasis on suppling the adductor muscles will help to improve the horse's lateral work. When a classically trained horse is laid off work, his muscles will usually become tight in one area more than in another. When bringing him back into work, the rider will have to concentrate more on the tight muscles than those which have become less tight.

The development of strength and power in dressage training through the accent on collection tends to work the horse's muscles in a small range of movement. Collected work puts strain on the hind leg flexors. With too much collection these muscles become strong, but too tight. They need to be suppled up regularly. Preserving suppleness while working towards collection and engagement is most important, as continual working in these small movement ranges can lead to repetitive stress injuries, and also to strain injuries when larger ranges of movement (such as in extended trot) are required. Training for power and strength alone will shorten and tighten the muscles, especially the hip flexors (iliopsoas), hence the importance of backward stretches. As we have already seen, losing suppleness in favour of strength and power leads to strain injuries. Strength and power are necessary, but not at the expense of suppleness. When performance or movement deteriorates in the dressage horse, the cause is often loss of suppleness. This can be a consequence of injury, enforced lay-off, or it may occur when the proven classical training programme is not adhered to. A programme of passive as well as active muscle stretching can prevent this.

Suppleness leads to a bigger range of movement and more agility. The increased range of movement leads to bigger and more beautiful strides and improves the extended gaits. A programme of passive stretching of the pectoral muscles and hind leg adductors, together with the suppling exercises of a classical training programme, will improve all lateral work. Stretching improves all lateral work by increasing the lateral stretch of the fore and hind legs and therefore improving the crossing over of the legs.

Extended trot, showing the stretching of the muscles.

Active stretching of the top line strengthens the abdominal muscles and helps to engage the hindquarters, thus helping to develop more push. As we shall see in Chapter 3, strong abdominal muscles improve all the gaits of the horse.

Racing

The ability of a horse to win races is dependent on a plethora of factors, including genetic factors, as well as the correct athletic training. Increased speed in racing is obtained by increasing the factors of stride length and stride frequency. The optimum influence of these factors may vary from horse to horse, but both can be positively influenced by stretch exercises. It has been proved that stride length is increased by training, especially through active stretch training. Active and passive stretching increase the stride length through the increased range of movement. A longer stride has a twofold effect on a racehorse's speed. In the first place, a longer stride allows the foot to linger longer on the ground and this produces more power and momentum. According to Dr Hilary Clayton, 'A limited range of motion is associated with an inferior ability to generate momentum and absorb impact forces'.[5] Secondly, the longer the stride, the more ground is covered.

The stride frequency can also be improved by stretching, as this increases the reflex response time through improved circulation and proprioception. Improved proprioception and balance enhance co-ordination, thus adding to the horse's racing ability.

Stretching exercises also play a major role in straightening the horse through suppling of the muscles. Because of their racing and training regime, many racehorses are fairly stiff to one side. This condition may be accentuated in countries or areas where all the courses run in the same direction (e.g. left-handed). If the horses are only worked and raced in one direction, this will exaggerate any natural stiffness to one side. The horse will then become increasingly more crooked. This crookedness will not only affect their ability to win races *in either direction*, but can also lead to injury. The reason why crookedness affects racing ability is as follows. A straight horse's weight will be distributed evenly over his hind legs. The energy produced by the hindquarters can thus be fully utilized to propel the horse forward in a straight line, maximizing speed and efficiency of movement. However, a crooked horse (regardless of the side to which he is crooked) will have to use more energy to achieve optimal stride length because the forelegs are not in line with the hind legs.

As racehorses are top-class athletes, they should be treated and trained in a balanced and scientific manner. No human athlete would consider training in only one direction. Athletes usually do endurance training, strength training in the gym and speed training. They also maintain their suppleness with regular stretch training. A stretch exercise programme will also contribute significantly to straight-

[5] Clayton, H.M., Training Showjumpers, in *The Athletic Horse. Principles and Practice of Equine Sports Medicine*, Hodgsen, D.R. and Rose, R.J. (eds.), W.B. Saunders Company (Philadelphia) 1994, p436.

ening the racehorse. When the horse is equally supple bilaterally, he should become straight in his movement.

The incidence of two fairly common strain injuries in racehorses, sacroiliac sprain/tear or sprain/tear of the superficial flexor tendons, can be reduced by keeping the racehorses supple with a daily stretch programme.

During a race, depending on the size of the horse, each front fetlock will be subjected to a force equivalent to 2–3 tons (2267–3174 kg) of weight.[6] The more flexible the fetlock becomes through stretch exercises and suppling of the leg flexor muscles and soft tissue, the more shock it can absorb and, as a consequence, the superficial and deep digital flexor tendons will be less likely to tear.

Racehorses in action. Note the hamstring stretch, the fetlock stretch and the quadriceps femoris stretch.

[6] Snow, Dr D.H. and Vogel, C.J., *Equine Fitness. The Care and Training of the Athletic Horse*, Trafalgar Square Farm Book, David and Charles, Inc. (North Pomfret) 1987, p.59.

Relaxation and Reduction of Muscle Tension, Stiffness and Anxiety

Tension is usually caused by physical or mental discomfort and is counter-productive to good performance. As in humans, the neck and back are usually the first areas to indicate tension in the horse. Thus stiffness, hollowness and physical tension in the dorsal chain (top line) can indicate anxiety and mental tension. By stretching the top line and placing the horse's head low the horse will become more relaxed and anxiety will be reduced. This is explained in detail in *Successful Schooling*. Basically, stretching of the neck reduces tension throughout the body, thereby improving the level of relaxation. Slow and gentle stretching of the neck, together with massage, have a relaxing effect on the whole horse.

Figure 4. Comparison of (a) an anxious, hollow outline with (b) a relaxed, rounded outline.

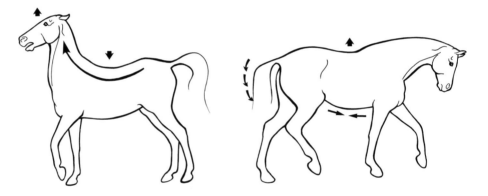

Causes of stiffness in the neck and back

An incorrect riding method

When the horse is not ridden in the correct round frame he will not strengthen the correct muscles (the abdominal muscles) and stretch the back. His back will be hollow and tense. Errors to avoid are:

1. Too strong a hold on the horse's mouth, with unyielding arms and hands. The horse pulls against this, to try to be free, using the incorrect muscles (neck and back extensors). This weakens the back and stiffens the neck and back.

2. Trying to *hold* the horse in a flexed position instead of *asking* for this position by allowing him to carry himself through yielding of the rider's arms and hands. When the horse is held in this way, he will set his neck by using the neck extensor group of muscles on top of the neck in concentric contraction, instead of using the neck flexors. This, again, will lead to tight neck muscles.

3. The back will become stiff when the horse 'sucks back' and shortens his neck by tightening his rhomboid and trapezius muscles. The little hollow area in front of the horse's withers is an indication that the horse is 'sucking back'. This is often caused or aggravated by a rider whose hands do not allow a stretching forward into the contact.

4. The incorrect use of running reins: tight running reins. The horse uses his back extensor muscles to pull against the tight running rein. This leads to tension, stiffness and hollowness. The neck can become so tight and painful that the horse cannot stretch to eat or drink for days. Running reins should hang loose when the horse is in the correct frame.

5. Riding the horse in the excessively deep and round frame can cause neck and back pain (see page 53).

6. Trying to lift the young horse's neck. It is seldom necessary to lift a horse's neck to a higher position. The horse will do this automatically as soon as he engages his hindquarters and collects himself. Attempting to lift the horse's head prematurely can cause discomfort, tension and stiffness.

Maltreatment

Emotional problems such as anxiety, tension or excitement will almost always present as stiffness in the back and neck. Because the horse is a prey animal, he has a well-developed startle reflex (fright/flight reflex), and this always produces a stiff and hollow neck and back. (See *Successful Schooling* for further explanation of the startle reflex.) His prey status also means that the horse is programmed never to forget previous attack or maltreatment. He may learn to trust his rider, but he is always ready to protect himself by going into the stiff 'ready to flee' stance. Incorrect muscular development and muscle spasms are often the result of tension associated with this instinctive response. For example, a tight noseband or an ill-fitting saddle can lead to defensive behaviour, manifest as resistance in the mouth and a stiff back and neck.

Trauma

Stiffness in the neck and back can be caused by traumatic incidents such as falls, kicking out at walls, and over-exuberance in the paddock. However, it should be borne in mind that activities such as jumping or performing advanced dressage movements (e.g. canter pirouettes) without warming up, can also lead to pain and stiffness in these areas.

Loss of balance

The neck is used as a powerful balancing mechanism. Muscles can go into spasm when the horse loses balance suddenly and the unprepared neck has to react quickly to maintain balance.

Straightening the Horse

There are two causes of crookedness in horses: dominance and the righting reaction.

Dominance

As is the case in humans, horses also have a dominant side and a non-dominant side: one side of the body is more difficult to bend than the other. The dominant side will always be stronger because horses are usually worked for only a relatively short period each day, so there will be many unridden hours in which they will automatically strengthen the dominant side, which they find easier to use. This is why it is so difficult for the rider to maintain straightness in a horse. The muscles of the dominant side are usually more developed than those of the non-dominant side and are therefore generally stronger, tighter and shorter. The non-dominant fore and hind leg will be weaker and usually more supple, and will therefore show a bigger range of movement than the dominant side. You will notice when you start the passive stretching exercises that the legs on one side will stretch further forward than on the other side. The stronger pair of legs will usually have the bigger muscles, but the shorter stride. The weaker legs will usually have a longer stride. It is more difficult for the horse to bend towards the non-dominant side because his neck muscles on the dominant side will be stronger, but shorter. To straighten the horse the dominant side muscles, especially, need to work through a daily stretch programme, while the weak side should be strengthened. These weak muscles can only strengthen in full when the short, opposing muscles have been stretched.

The righting reaction

This reaction is explained in depth in *Successful Schooling*. Basically, the righting reaction is the desire of the body to stay in alignment with the central nervous system (the head and spine). When an animal's (or human's) head is turned to one side, the shoulders, followed by the hips, will turn in the same direction. When an animal's head is bent forwards, his back will round, followed by the waist area flexing and then the hips flexing as well. The opposite will happen if the head is bent backwards: the back will hollow and the hips will hyper-extend. This is an automatic reaction of the body to protect itself. This reaction is clearly illustrated when a horse is tense and keeps his head and neck rigid. This will lead to the body also becoming rigid.

Results of the righting reaction can be seen in the crooked and swinging quarters of the horse during flying changes, the quarters falling out in the shoulder-in and the quarters falling out when you spiral in from a circle. If the horse is tense in the counter-canter, he will break into a trot or do an unauthorized flying change because of the influence of this righting reaction. Fortunately, teaching the horse to yield instantly to light pressure on the reins can inhibit this righting reaction. When the horse yields perfectly to the rider's hands through his flying changes, the changes will be straight The quarters will not fall out in the shoulder-in when the horse yields to the rider's inside hand, neither will the quarters fall out when riding a spiral if the horse's neck and mouth yield perfectly to the rider's inside hand. This is also the reason why a horse should be ridden from the inside leg to the outside hand, and why turns and the shoulder-in are controlled with the outside hand, not the inside hand. (Although inhibiting the righting reaction will prevent the quarters from swinging or falling in or out, it cannot fix other flaws, errors or faults of the movements.)

Some instructors use the effect of this righting reaction to straighten the horse. They use counter-flexion to bend the horse to the outside. By using a firm contact on the outside rein, the neck will not be yielding to the rider's outside hand, but 'pulling' against it. The horse's neck will thus be rigid. The righting reaction will then automatically lead to rigidity of the horse's back, which will move into alignment with his neck, thus bringing the horse's hindquarters to the inside of the circle. When the rider puts the horse back on the inside bend, with a soft feel on the inside rein, his hind legs will follow the track of the forelegs. However, if the rider does not maintain this soft feel on the inside rein, or if the horse does not yield perfectly to the rider's inside hand, the solution will only be temporary. Suppling/stretch exercises will allow the horse to yield to the rider's inside hand and inhibit the righting reaction, and this will then have a permanent straightening effect.

Figure 5. The righting reaction. When the horse is pulled in by the inside rein the righting reaction, which maintains the alignment of the head and spine, will move the hindquarters out of the circle (continuous line). When the horse yields perfectly to the inside, with his inside neck muscles contracting, the righting reaction is inhibited and the hindquarters will maintain the bend and the hind feet will step into the hoofprints of the forefeet.

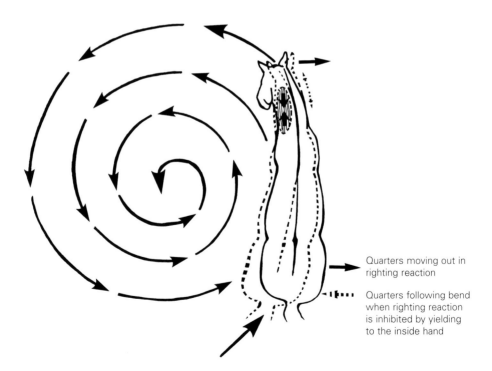

Quarters moving out in righting reaction

Quarters following bend when righting reaction is inhibited by yielding to the inside hand

When the horse is straight, his weight is distributed evenly. He thus shows better balance, the energy comes through and the movement becomes freer and more graceful. The horse becomes easier to ride and the advanced movements are easier to perform. Straightness leads to more gymnastic ability. In a crooked horse, the energy remains 'locked in.'

Improving Submission

Removing physical resistance, such as stiff muscles in the neck, enables the horse to stay on the bit without discomfort and thus become more submissive. Some horses find it difficult to stay on the bit: the nuchal ligament may be relatively short or there may be actual spasm in an opposing muscle. The consequent discomfort prevents the horse from listening to the rider's commands. Although such a horse may appear to be disobedient to the rider's commands, it can be pain or discomfort that is causing this particular resistance. By doing stretching exercises, many of these resistances can be removed and the horse will then accept a steady contact with greater ease. It is worth noting that lack of submission in other areas (for example, resistance to lateral work) may also be a sign of physical stiffness rather than actual disobedience.

Figure 6. Submission and resistance. (a) The frame rounded in submission. (b) The tight top line muscles of resistance.

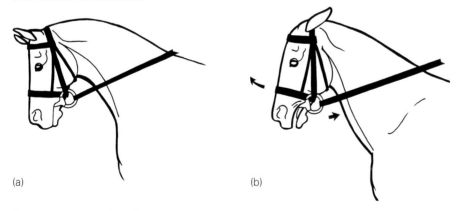

(a)   (b)

Improving Rideability

A supple horse is a more comfortable ride. Three factors contribute towards greater comfort.

1. A stiff, hollow back produces a very uncomfortable trot, bouncing the rider right out of the saddle. The rider will therefore find it very difficult to develop a deep seat and to move with the horse. By stretching the top line and contracting the bottom line abdominal muscles, the horse's back becomes more pliant, soft and comfortable. The arching of the back is initiated by the rounding of the neck. The more flexible the back muscles, the more the abdominal muscles can contract to produce this soft, arched back.

2. The angles and flexibility of the leg joints. The horse has angles at his fetlock, hock, stifle and hip joints (elbow and shoulder joints in the forelimbs). These angles increase the capacity of the horse's legs for shock absorption, thereby making the 'bounce' in the back more comfortable for the rider. The more flexible these leg joints, the more shock absorption is possible. Supple hind fetlock joints especially produce a very comfortable trot. However, when these joints are stiff and inflexible, the trot will almost catapult the rider out of the saddle. This may be particularly noticeable if a stiff-jointed horse is asked to perform extended trot, when even a talented rider may find sitting to the trot is too uncomfortable. However, by improving the mobility of the joints and stretching the muscles in the legs, more cushioning and shock absorption is produced. Stretching exercises will improve the mobility of the joints and muscles. These attributes will lead to a more comfortable horse, especially at the sitting trot. Thus a daily stretching programme can improve even a naturally uncomfortable horse.

3. Another factor that contributes to comfort as well as performance is the ability of the horse to engage his hind legs. Increased flexibility of the hind leg extensor muscles (gluteal muscles) allows the hind legs to move more underneath the horse (produce more engagement).

Increasing Weight-bearing Capacity.

Riding a horse in a stiff, hollow frame can lead to his back becoming painful and may put too much stress on the leg joints. By stretching the back, the abdominal muscles will automatically contract. Strong abdominal muscles are the main supporters of the vertebral column and are completely necessary for strengthening the back and increasing weight-bearing capacity. Therefore strengthening the abdominal muscles through stretching the top line muscles will enhance the weight-bearing capacity and thus contribute to preventing back injury. The stronger the abdominal muscles, the better the weight-bearing capacity. Exercises to stretch the horse's back in-hand before mounting will prepare it for the displacement caused by the weight of the rider (see page 82).

Figure 7. Strengthening the abdominal muscles will improve weight-bearing capacity. (a) Hollow back with weak abdominal muscles; (b) rounded back with strong abdominal muscles.

(a)　　　　　　　　　　　　　　(b)

CHAPTER 2

Basic Anatomy
and Physiology

How Muscles Work to Produce Movement

Skeletal muscles come in many shapes and sizes, but they all have the same basic functions of maintaining posture and producing skeletal movement. When they contract in concentric contraction, they bring one bone closer to another or they stabilize one joint while moving another.

The bulk of a skeletal muscle consists of a fleshy middle part, which merges into a tendon at each end. This, in turn, attaches the muscle to the bone by way of the periosteum. Muscles are mainly made up of thousands of muscle cells (muscle fibres). These muscle cells are composed of contractile proteins in the form of myofibrils which lie parallel to each other. Within these myofibrils is a repeating unit of myofilaments, which are called sarcomeres, the fundamental contractile elements of the muscles. These myofilaments of primary protein, called actin (thin filaments) and myosin (thick filaments) overlap each other. When the muscle contracts, the filaments slide over each other, thereby shortening the muscle. When the muscle relaxes, the filaments return to their original position and the muscle lengthens again.

Each muscle fibre (muscle cell) is surrounded by connective tissue known as endomysium. These muscle cells are grouped in bundles and each bundle is surrounded in turn by more connective tissue (the perimysium). A group of muscle bundles is again surrounded by connective tissue and this bundle of bundles forms the muscle itself. The connective tissue from all these groups merges to become the tendons at each end of the muscle. This arrangement of the connective tissue surrounding each fibre, each bundle, and the muscle itself, increases elasticity and strength of the muscle. The connective tissue around the muscle itself is called the muscle sheath or epimysium.

Figure 8. Muscle anatomy.

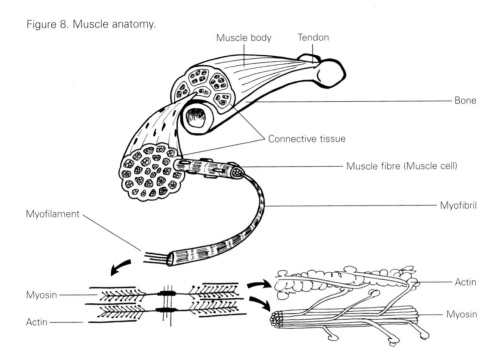

There are two types of muscle fibre which define the athletic characteristics of an individual. Type I, the slow-twitch fibre, has high resistance to fatigue. Horses with predominantly slow-twitch muscle fibres are more suited to endurance and dressage work. Type II, the fast-twitch fibres, give the muscles maximum strength and speed, but have low resistance to fatigue. Horses with predominantly fast-twitch fibres are more suited to sprinting and showjumping.

The difference in the size of muscles relates to the difference in the cell numbers (the more cells, the bigger the muscle) as well as to the size of each muscle cell. However, the number of cells in most muscles is fixed around the time of birth and does not change much during the animal's lifetime. When the muscles are strengthened the fibres grow bigger and thus this sheath becomes fuller, producing a larger and firmer body. Since the fibres are elastic, they can stretch and compress again. When the fibres are strengthened through repetitive contraction without sufficient opportunity to stretch, they become shorter and tighter and their ability to stretch decreases. This situation is, however, reversible through a programme of stretching/suppling.

The tendons serve to anchor the muscle onto the bones and to transfer muscular activity to the bone. They anchor by becoming continuous with the periosteum of the bone. The tendons themselves do not possess much elasticity. The muscles are the elastic part of this movement apparatus. When the tendon stretches over the joint it

Figure 9. The actions of the agonist and antagonist spanning the joint, shown in the human arm.(a) Contraction of biceps – relaxation of triceps, closing the joint to bring the two bones closer together in flexion.

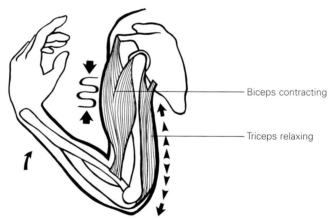

Biceps contracting

Triceps relaxing

(b) Contraction of triceps – relaxation of biceps, opening the joint to move the bones further apart in extension.

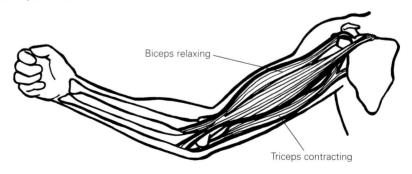

Biceps relaxing

Triceps contracting

is dependent on the muscle itself to stretch. If the muscle cannot stretch sufficiently, the tendon will become injured, or even tear off its bony attachment .

The skeletal muscles are attached to a bone at each end. The proximal (top) attachment is usually called the origin while the distal (bottom) attachment is called the insertion. In between two bones will be a joint. All active movement is dependent on the contraction of a muscle. When the muscle contracts it pulls the bone to which its insertion is attached in the direction of its origin. In some cases, one muscle will have two functions as a consequence of having attachment onto two bones, or when it spans two joints. The very large muscle on the underside of the horse's neck, the brachiocephalicus, spans two joints and thus has two functions: it is responsible for the forward movement of the horse's foreleg, but when the foreleg is stationary, this same muscle will turn the horse's head sideways.

Muscles usually work in synergistic groups to produce complex movement patterns. These groups of muscles that work together are called agonists. The group of muscles on the opposite side of the joint, producing the opposite movement, are called the antagonists. When an agonist contracts the antagonist must relax to allow full contraction of the agonist. The antagonist should therefore be very flexible and supple to allow full contraction of the agonist. During active stretching exercises with the horse, synergistic groups of muscles are stretched, thus enhancing flexibility and suppleness. Muscle contraction is released by slow relaxation of the muscle fibres.

Muscles are the most adaptable of all the body tissues. They are able to change in size, becoming bigger or smaller, longer or shorter. Of all the body tissues except for the skin, muscles are also the most able to regenerate, being capable of so doing from the intact ends when the fibres are partly destroyed.[1]

A few differences between the equine and human muscular systems should be mentioned. The horse's normal temperature is higher than the human's (approximately 100.5 °F as opposed to 98.4 °F). His normal pulse rate is lower than that of his human counterpart (22–55 as opposed to approximately 72) and his heart-lung capacity is bigger in relation to his body mass than a human's. Therefore the exertion-recovery time of the horse's muscles is faster than that of the human because the waste products of metabolism are removed faster. A human loses fitness within a week of ceasing training, while the horse takes two weeks to lose his fitness. The

[1] Lockhart, R.D., Hamilton, G.F. and Fyfe F.W., *Anatomy of the Human Body*, Faber and Faber Ltd. (London) 1965.

horse also regains fitness faster after a rest period than the human athlete does. However, compared to horses, humans have far greater possibilities of movement patterns. New dance steps are constantly being choreographed and acrobatic dancers or artists can literally fold themselves 'in half'. Horses, however, have limited movement patterns because of anatomical restrictions. It is probable that all the different movement patterns possible in horses have already been investigated. Over the centuries very few new movements have been created. Notable innovators have been François de la Guérinière, who devised the shoulder-in during the eighteenth century, François Baucher, the first rider to perform one-time flying changes during the nineteenth century and Gabriella Grillo, who made the combination of the walk pirouette with the canter pirouette famous during the 1980s.

The muscles are innervated by two important nerve cells: (a) the muscle spindle nerve cells, and (b) the Golgi apparatus nerve cells.

The Muscle Spindle and the Stretch Reflex

Coiled around each muscle fibre is a muscle spindle cell. This muscle spindle is extremely sensitive to any stretch in the muscle fibre. The spindle cell tries to protect the muscle fibre from overstretch or strain. As soon as the spindle cell perceives a stretch that may damage the muscle fibre, it sends a signal to the brain, which instructs it to contract. A strong and fast stretch will thus trigger an automatic contraction to protect the muscle fibres from injury caused by overstretch and tearing of the fibres. To override this reflex, the muscle has to be elongated slowly and smoothly and a mild stretch maintained for 5–15 seconds or more. As soon as some of the tension is released the stretch can be increased slowly again and maintained.

Figure 10. A muscle spindle cell.

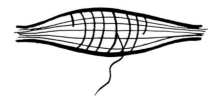

The Golgi Apparatus

The Golgi nerve cells are situated mainly in the areas where the muscle body meets the tendon. They serve to inform the brain as to the whereabouts of the muscles and, therefore, the limbs. If you close your eyes you will immediately know where your body parts are and what they are doing, courtesy of these nerve cells. This is the proprioception mentioned earlier, which is important for body awareness, body schema, balance and co-ordination. The Golgi cells are also responsible for the body's kinesthetic sense – the 'feel' of movement.

CHAPTER 3

The Fundamentals of Stretching

The Three Forms of Stretching

There are three forms of muscle stretching that are used to improve athletic ability and prevent injury. These are active stretching, passive stretching and using the automatic reflex reactions.

Active Stretching

With this method the horse does his own stretching with the guidance of the rider. That is to say, the horse is mounted and specific stretch exercises are performed on a daily basis throughout the horse's career. The muscles stretch actively when the opposing muscles contract. During active contraction of the synergists, a neural impulse is sent to the antagonists, which makes them relax, thereby allowing them to stretch. This method is safer than passive stretching as the horse will automatically protect himself from injury by way of the stretch reflex. The rider should, however, be careful not to *force* the horse's movement as this could still lead to injury. Examples of such forcing include too much work in collected gaits, too sharp an angle in the half-pass too early in training, or jumping too high for the horse's level of fitness.

Active stretching exercises should be incorporated in all horses' daily workout programmes. They should form an integral part of the warm-up to prepare the muscles for work. After the horse's work session the muscles should be elongated again to relax the horse. If the muscles are not elongated after collected work, the horse will lose suppleness and be susceptible to stress injuries.

Passive Stretching

This method is performed off the horse by a hands-on approach. The handler physically moves the limb slowly through its entire range of movement, thereby inhibiting the stretch reflex. When the limit of the range is reached the position is maintained for 5–15 seconds to ensure permanent lengthening. If the stretch is not held, the muscles, tendons and ligaments will revert back to their original length. (See Ground Rules for Stretching Muscles below, for further details.) The movement should be performed slowly to avoid the reflexive muscular contraction triggered by fast, excessive stretching. If this work is not performed carefully, applying knowledge and experience, it can lead to muscle or tendon injury. Great care should be taken to prevent this. These passive stretch exercises should be performed daily *after* the horse's workout.

Automatic Reactions

A few automatic reactions can be used to induce stretch in certain parts of the horse. By touching the horse in certain areas, specific automatic contractions can be elicited. An example of an automatic reaction is the balance reaction. If you disturb an animal's balance he will automatically adjust his body in order not to lose his balance and fall over. The animal does not have to think of this reaction, it simply happens.

Ground Rules for Stretching Muscles

Active Stretching

* Active stretching should be carried out as part of the warm-up period, before new work or the main workout is tackled. Before starting active stretching exercises do 5–10 minutes warm-up with active forward movement in walk, trot or canter. Stretching should only be performed once the horse is relaxed: attempting to achieve stretch in a tense horse will be counter-productive and can lead to injury. Also do some stretching exercises to relax the muscles after collected work and jumping and at the end of the work session, in order that the muscles can regain their resting length.

* Once basic suppleness has developed, power and suppling exercises should be done, where possible, in parallel. As previously explained, suppleness without

strength can lead to instability of the joints, while power without suppleness can lead to muscle and tendon injuries.

- Lateral stretching is more effective if done at the walk (shoulder-in, leg-yield, etc. – see Chapter 4).

- Longitudinal stretching over ground poles should be done at walk as well as at trot to achieve different results.

Passive Stretching

- Passive stretching can be dangerous and can cause injury if performed incorrectly. It is very much preferable that anyone seeking to carry out passive stretching should first gain experience by observing and being guided by a qualified therapist. If this is not possible, start with very small passive stretches such as the rotations (see page 43 – also pages 105–7).

- It is not advised that children under the age of 13 do the passive stretching exercises with horses, but older children are quite capable of doing these exercises if trained carefully.

- Overstretching in hyper-flexion or hyper-extension can cause muscle injury. Be guided by your horse – know him and be in tune with him. Any sign of discomfort should be acknowledged with a release of the stretch. Head throwing, ears set backwards, resistance in the jaw, resistance against the leg or refusing to jump (this could be a tight hamstring), are all signs of discomfort. Overstretching can cause tightening, which will be followed by muscle spasm. This can only be released by deep massage or acupuncture. Never force the stretch. Forcing a muscle in spasm can lead to tearing of tissue or a pulled muscle.

- The horse should not be stretched during or after rest periods, illness, injury, or post-operatively until he is healed. Any rehabilitative stretching should be done under strict medical guidance. Consult the veterinarian and physiotherapist should lameness appear when doing rehabilitative stretching. Never stretch a painful muscle. Painful resistance to stretching should be a warning to seek medical assistance. Only once the horse has fully recovered should you start to reintroduce the normal stretching regime with slow and small stretches.

- Rather do too little than too much. A horse's muscles start to stretch within 5 seconds whereas a human's muscles only start to stretch after 30 seconds. When starting the stretch programme, stretch for only 5 seconds and build up gradually to 15 seconds. If the stretch is held for too long, the blood supply to the nerves may be compromised, leading to increased tension in the muscles, and even painful cramps. Never hold the stretch for more than 20 seconds.

- Before starting passive stretches, be aware of what is a normal stretch range. (Photographs that accompany text on the individual exercises in Chapter 4 illustrate this.) Always start with small stretches and increase the movements slowly within the horse's comfort zone, otherwise you may inadvertently stretch beyond what is normal for horses. This can lead to destabilizing of the joints.

- Stretching should be specific to each individual horse's needs. One horse may be especially tight in the adductors while another may have great freedom of movement in that area, which allows for superior lateral stretch as demonstrated in his half-passes. When a horse has particularly tight muscles the stretch should start out being very small and very slow. A particular horse's need for stretching may differ from time to time in his career, perhaps as a consequence of injury or illness. Adjust your programme accordingly.

- Passive stretching should be done only after the workout, on warm muscles and tendons in a calm environment, to promote relaxation and release contracture or tightness built up from the collected work. Stretching can cause injury if performed on cold muscles. Stretch after at least 15 minutes warm-up in walk, trot or canter, but do not stretch more than 30 minutes after the exercise has ceased. Through movement, when the horse is warmed up, the coloidial gel in the soft tissue becomes liquid and jelly-like in substance, thus allowing the different tissues to glide over each other (for example, superficial muscle over deep muscle; tendon over bone). When cold, this gel is tacky and sticky and therefore allows for more friction between soft tissue layers and bones. Also, in the warmed-up horse, increased blood flow to the musculoskeletal tissues increases the local temperature and improves the viscoelastic properties of muscles and joints, Additionally, energy supply and waste product removal are improved, and nerve control/proprioception is enhanced.

- For passive stretching, protective gloves may be worn, but these have to provide a good grip to ensure that the horse's feet do not slip.

Practical Basics of Stretch Exercises

The Therapist's Posture during Passive Stretching

Your own posture is important while you are stretching the horse. Poor posture and body alignment can injure your back and cause muscle strain. The horse is large and heavy and initially does not give his full co-operation to the stretching processes. Never use your back to carry the horse's weight. Centre your weight and use your entire body to lift your horse's leg or to rotate it. Drop your centre of gravity by broadening your base of support, bending your knees and placing your feet apart, one slightly in front of the other. This will give you more power and manoeuvrability and transfer the effort from your back to your thighs. Use your thigh and abdominal muscles instead of your back muscles. Try not to use your arms and hands only, as this may injure the muscles of your shoulder girdle. Rest your elbow on your knee whenever possible to save your back. Try to keep your back as straight as possible and use your weight rather than your muscles to stretch the horse – this will give you more power, but also more protection for your back. Try to avoid tension in your shoulders, arms and hands while working.

Preparatory Practice for Passive Stretching

Acquiring a new skill is often a daunting task. Learning a technique from a book, without a personal demonstration, is even more difficult and many people start out with good intentions, but are put off when they are not immediately successful.

A good way to start learning how to do passive stretching exercises is to begin straight after dismounting and removing the tack. Simply pick up each limb, one at a time and hold it without trying to stretch it. Try to maintain the hold for 5 seconds. Do not expect to gain confidence immediately. Repeat this for a few days. By this time the horse should lift his foot as you take up position next to each leg. Once the horse accepts standing on three legs, you may start with small rotations of the limbs. These rotations are safe, mild, and easy to perform and will give you a good introduction to the technique. (The rotations may not be necessary once you have mastered the stretching technique and the horse is being stretched in all the directions. However, should the horse be off work for some time, then commence the stretch exercises with rotations again.)

Once you have mastered the rotations, try a mild forward stretch. Hold the first stretch for 5 seconds. Replace each leg in its original position. Increase the range of the stretches slowly until your confidence grows, then try the more difficult backward and lateral stretches described in Chapter 4. Try to get the feel of the difference between resistance and normal movement. Only when you know the correct feel should you stretch the muscles to their full capacity.

It may take up to two weeks to learn the routine. During this time especially, it is far safer to be ineffective in your stretching than to overstretch or to hold the stretch for too long. Choose one exercise at a time and practise it until you feel comfortable with it, then try a new one. Go through all the stretch exercises until you find those which suit your horse the most. Add other stretches when necessary or change them completely as needed.

General Principles of Passive Stretching

Passive stretching is not as easy as an experienced practitioner may make it appear. Horses are not over-fond of standing on three legs and having their balance disturbed. Therefore you need to work very gently and be careful not to disturb a horse's balance until he happily accepts standing on three legs and allows you to hold him in a position for 5–15 seconds.

The stretch exercises described in this book will demonstrate one way of stretching. As you become more familiar with the stretches, you may find a different way, which will suit you better. So long as you do not change the horse's position, you may place your hands, legs or body differently for more comfort.

Always approach the horse gently, whether he is anxious or not. Stroke the horse first to relax him. Slide your hands down the appropriate leg and then ask him to lift the limb by pinching the tendon behind his cannon bone (superficial flexor tendon), or else pinch the chestnut. Support the limb with both hands from the moment it is picked up, through the stretch and while you are returning it to its original position. Do not drop it. This will give the horse the security to trust you, to co-operate and not to retract the limb.

Stretch and release slowly and gradually and use slow, fluid movements with no jerking, to prevent spasm or injury. If the stretching is done fast and with too much force the muscles will revert back to their previous length because of the stretch reflex and the stretch will have been of no use. Fast, forceful stretching can also cause muscle strain injuries. Always start with moderate stretching and when the horse accepts the small stretches, slowly increase the range. Gradual stretching and holding for longer periods will have a more permanent effect. Stretch until resistance is felt, or the horse shows discomfort, but do not force it. From the position of discomfort, release the stretch a little and hold for 5–15 seconds. If a stretch is to be effective it should be held for 5–15 seconds after the horse has relaxed since this timescale should bypass the stretch reflex. To measure the seconds, simply count them out slowly.

Do not overstretch, as this will trigger the stretch reflex. Also, note that the muscles should not be 'bounced' by shaking the limb at the end of the movement range. This will increase muscle tone instead of decreasing it as is required when stretching.

At the end of the allotted time, release the limb slowly and replace it gently in its original position. Change sides frequently to prevent fatigue.

You may repeat each stretch three times, but will probably find that once only is sufficiently time-consuming. End a stretching session with a relaxing tail stretch (see pages 86–7).

Stretching exercises should be performed daily, at first to increase the range of movement and, once this is achieved, to maintain the optimum range of movement. Therefore, try to make a habit of stretching daily after removing the tack. If you can't make a habit of it you will probably give up altogether. However, you need not go through the whole repertoire of stretches every day. The amount of stretching depends on each horse's individual needs – for instance, some horses may have adequate longitudinal suppleness, but lack lateral suppleness. Therefore, choose the appropriate stretches to do. Check regularly to ascertain where most stretch is necessary. You will find that all horses tend to be more flexible on one side than the other. Compare the two sides when stretching. The aim is to even them out and straighten the horse. Each horse's needs may also change from time to time. It may be necessary to stretch a specific area for a short period, but once this area is loosened up, it may not need more passive stretching. Active stretching may maintain it sufficiently.

Significant improvement in the passive range of movement should be noticed after one month. In the case of horses with very short strides, you should start noticing an improvement in the stride length after a few weeks.

Stretching the Young Horse

Human gymnasts start from a young age with exercises to maintain their natural suppleness. If you start stretch exercises with the horse too late, his muscles may have become tighter and this elasticity is far more difficult to regain than to maintain. However, introducing this work needs to be done carefully, with due consideration of some important points.

The young horse's muscles are undeveloped and lack muscle tone, but they are more supple and flexible than those of the older horse. However, the young horse's tendons and ligaments are also a lot looser than the older horse's and therefore the joints may have less stability. Overstretching or starting passive stretch exercises too early in training may lead to destabilizing of the joints. Stretching should thus be less vigorous in order to protect the joints. If the back is stretched too early the vertebrae may become too pliable, loose and unstable and therefore not able to form a strong base for the limbs to move against. So, for the first few months, the young horse should not work in too low and round a frame. He should be given only light work. In fact, active stretching is more applicable than passive stretching during this time.

The abdominal muscles should be strengthened first through working in walk and trot up and down hills and slopes. General exercise such as hacking is important during this stage, although suppleness in all directions should be maintained from early on, as horses' muscles are more pliable when they are young. Maintain this natural suppleness with active stretch (ridden) exercises. *All the muscle groups have to be worked through an active stretch programme.* I emphasize this point because there seems to be a general misconception in certain riding circles that lateral work should be started later in the training. A human gymnast would not consider maintaining or improving suppleness in one area while leaving the other areas to become tight. However, we often find that young horses' suppleness is only maintained in the longitudinal plane of movement and not in the lateral plane. A horse will naturally move his legs in all directions, not only forward and backward. Suppleness in all directions should thus be maintained from relatively early in training to prevent the natural tightness from setting in. Do not be afraid to do lateral work at the walk with the young horse. Start with lateral exercises as soon as the horse moves forward in balance and rhythm. If you start early you will not lose this wonderful, natural, lateral suppleness. As young horses have such natural suppleness, you only need to go through the exercises at walk, but you need not push for a much bigger stretch to maintain this suppleness. As the horse's strength develops, you can ask for bigger lateral steps.

It is important to recognize that the young horse has to develop a strong abdominal girdle before starting counter-canter because counter-canter involves contracting the relevant muscles in their outer range of movement, and muscle action is easiest and most efficient in its mid-range of movement. This matter is discussed further in Chapter 4 – Active Stretch Exercises for the Lateral Flexors of the Trunk.

Stretching the Older Horse

The older horse's muscles, ligaments and tendons become less flexible (tighter) over time and will need more stretching than those of the young horse. He will need daily active and passive stretch exercises – especially the lateral stretch exercises – or he will lose suppleness. His muscles will need to be warmed up and stretched before the start of every vigorous work session. The warm-up session should take account of the fact that an older horse will take longer to become supple, and be more prone to stretch injury, than a younger horse, and he may also start off with a greater degree of stable stiffness. It is, nevertheless, still feasible to make an older horse very supple through a slow, diligent programme of stretching.

CHAPTER 4

The Stretching Exercises

If stretching is to be used as an effective means of preparing the horse for his work, it has to incorporate all the muscle groups involved in all the basic movement patterns. When a horse moves in a specific direction, a group of muscles work together (synergistically). Some muscles have several roles, for example, the medial gluteus extends and abducts the joint. You will notice that such muscles are mentioned in more than one stretch exercise, because their varying roles place them in more than one synergistic group. (In this context, it is interesting to note a contrast between horses and humans. Whereas the human body can often isolate movement to a specific muscle because of the nature of the muscle attachments, this ability is less prevalent in horses. For example, while humans can flex and extend the knee and heel independently, the horse's stifle and hock always flex and extend simultaneously as a function of the reciprocal apparatus. This interaction limits the diversity of movement patterns and passive stretch patterns in the horse.)

All the *passive* stretch exercises detailed in this chapter are described as performed from the horse's near (left) side. Repeat each exercise on the off (right) side as well. For ease of reference, many of the *active* stretch exercises are repeated in the different sections.

The Head and Neck

The entire spine should be treated as one single system. It is difficult to isolate one part and not have an effect on the rest. For instance, stiffness in the neck will produce stiffness in the back. This is because of the effect of the righting reactions as well as the layering of the origins and insertions of the muscles along the spine (the longissimus and the multifidus dorsi muscles) and the nuchal apparatus. That is the reason why the neck and trunk muscles work in synergy in two chains, the dorsal chain (top line) and the ventral chain (bottom line).

Muscle Chains

The dorsal muscle chain
This consists of:
1. The neck extensors on the top of the neck which lift the neck and extend the cervico-thoracic joint.
2. The back extensors and the juxta-vertebral muscles which 'hollow' the back.
3. The hip extensors are the gluteal and hamstring muscles, which are the major propulsive muscles.

The dorsal chain is responsible for impulsion, jumping and leaping, and plays an important role in the canter. It lifts up the forehand through the interconnections of the muscles and the nuchal apparatus, which is the strong ligament that runs from the head to the tail, connecting all the vertebrae. From the stifle, the muscles pull on the pelvis, from the pelvis they pull on the trunk and from the trunk they pull on the withers and neck to lift the forehand. Through these attachments they hold the entire horse against the pull of gravity when the forelimbs are off the ground. Therefore, discomfort during the canter is usually a sign of a painful back or a painful hindquarter. The horse will usually show the discomfort by throwing his head or pulling/hanging on the bit. When the horse is hard in the hands these muscles are not stretching, but actually contracting. Stretching these muscles will enable the horse to stay in the 'on the bit' position with greater ease.

Tightness in the dorsal chain is often caused by incorrect riding methods – unyielding hands in too strong contact, or active lifting of the neck when seeking a higher neck carriage, instead of pushing from behind to achieve true collection and engagement, which will bring the neck up naturally. By lifting the neck with the hands instead of pushing with the legs, the rider causes the horse's back flexors and neck extensors to work against each other unnaturally. This can cause gait abnormalities such as pacing or shuffling in the collected walk.

Figure 11. The interconnection of muscles which constitute the dorsal (top line) and ventral (bottom line) chains.

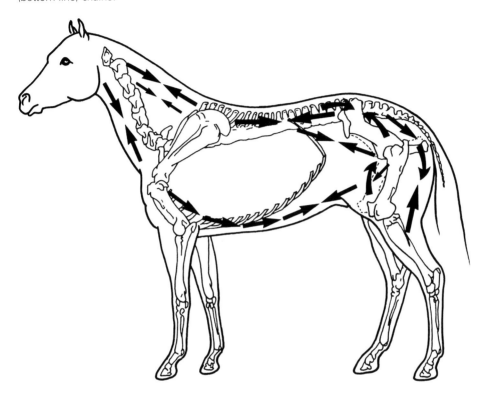

The ventral muscle chain

This consists of:

1. The neck flexors on the underside of the neck.
2. The abdominal muscles which flex or arch the back.
3. The hip and lumbo-sacral flexors.

This bottom line supports and strengthens the back, is the 'power chain' and produces engagement of the hindquarters through the contraction of the abdominal muscles, hip flexors and the quadriceps femoris muscle, which flexes the hip and extends the stifle and hock joints. When a hind leg is placed on the ground, the quadriceps muscle has to extend the stifle and pull the horse's body over the leg. When the leg is perpendicular to the ground in the stance phase, the hamstrings and gluteal muscles contract to propel the body further over the horse. The carrying power of the quadriceps femoris muscle is important for sustaining engagement in the collected movements such as piaffe, passage, canter pirouettes and when jumping and also in extended trot. Because the spine works as a unit in flexion and extension, the cervical (neck) section works in synergy with the abdominal section and thus has an influence on lumbar flexion and engagement. When the neck flexes down and round, the back will arch, bringing the pelvis towards the sternum, and the hips will flex, thus becoming more engaged. For this reason, many of the active stretch exercises for the neck will be repeated in the other sections on stretching.

Figure 12. When the neck flexes down and round, the back arches.

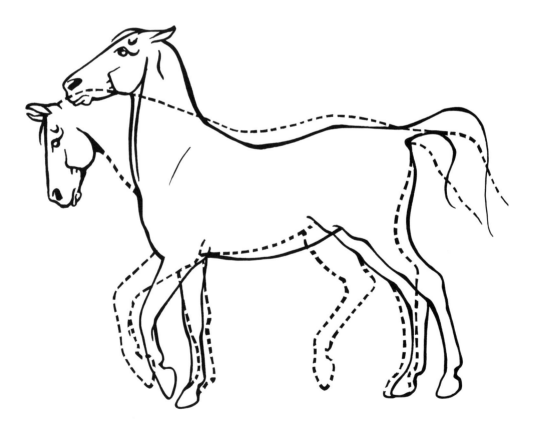

The neck muscles are very important for both locomotion and balance. The horse uses the weight of his neck as a balancing mechanism for the rest of his body. This is noticeable in transitions when he lifts his neck to maintain balance. In his natural state he stretches it forwards in the gallop or canter and, when he stops, he lifts it up when he braces his forelegs. He also lifts it when initiating movement. These actions move his centre of gravity backwards and forwards. It is said that Secretariat's greatness on the racetrack was partly due to his ability to stretch his neck forwards during each stride of the gallop.

Since the neck – and, by extension, the back – play such important roles in the horse's movement, it is evident that suppleness of these areas should be maintained throughout the horse's career. A supple neck and back are essential to producing optimal movement in the horse. All stiffness in the neck or back will have a negative effect on the horse's movement.

Stretching the Neck and Head Extensors – Downward Stretch

Stretching the dorsal muscle chain (top line) mobilizes the vertebral joints and renders them more flexible. When the neck is more flexible better quality of movement is possible and overall balance will improve since, as we have seen, the neck plays a major role in maintaining the horse's balance. These factors will make significant contributions to improving both jumping ability and speed. Many of the advantages in terms of dressage work will be self-evident, but there are also significant benefits that may be less obvious. For example, when the neck is relaxed and down, the vertebrae can rotate more easily during the diagonal movement of the trot. This helps the hips and hindquarters to move with greater ease and makes the horse more comfortable.

This flexor pattern helps to inhibit the fright muscle pattern (hollow) or startle reflex, and thus plays an important role in relaxing the horse. Additionally, this position diminishes the horse's field of vision somewhat, effectively helping him to concentrate and relax. With the neck stretched down and round, the flexion righting reaction is set in motion. This produces contraction of the flexor muscles, thus arching the back, and helps to bring the hindquarters more underneath the horse. The bottom line muscles can only strengthen and give more stability to the back when the neck stretches down.

51

As the nuchal ligament is elastic[1], it appears to have the ability to lengthen. So far as the top line is concerned, horses with short nuchal ligaments and top line muscles need regular, but careful, stretching of the top line. Signs of a short nuchal ligament are:

A hollow area in front of the withers.

A straight top line.

Tight top line muscles with a high, hollow neck carriage.

A difficulty in stretching long and low despite correct training.

The apparent slipping of the crest from one side to the other, as the horse bends his neck, is actually the tight nuchal ligament. Shortening is often caused by injury, and may be accompanied by thickening, which is visible to the naked eye. Where these signs are evident, professional advice should be sought regarding physiotherapy.

Types of exercise

Three types of active stretches for the neck extensor muscles can be defined. These are:

Long and low. The neck is carried low, with the nose close to the ground. The head and neck form a continuous bottom line, with the angle between the jaw and the neck open. This is a good stretch of the top line from poll to dock and it has the added advantage of giving the horse the opportunity to stretch his head-on-neck flexor muscles under his jaw. This stretch should always follow periods of collection, during which the horse has to work in a shortened frame. The horse should be ridden on a long rein with a soft contact and no pull on the mouth.

Low and round. In this position, the horse is still in a long frame, stretching down to the ground. However, because of the position of his neck, the head will be behind the vertical – although he will not be behind the bit. This has a stronger stretch effect on the top line, since the horse's head and neck extensor muscles will be stretching.

[1] Smythe, R.H. and Goody, P.C., *The Horse Structure and Movement*, J.A. Allen (London) 1988.

Figure 13. (a) Long and low; (b) low and round; (c) deep and round.

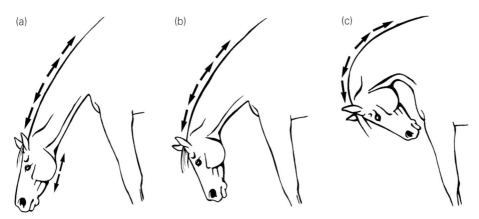

Deep and round. In this position, the neck is curled round so that the nose reaches the horse's chest. This position is neither physically nor psychologically advantageous to the horse, and the ethics of using it are highly questionable. Unfortunately, it is, at present, practised and advocated by some riders and trainers. Those who use this method often maintain the position for 10 minutes or so. However, scientific reviews indicate that such a position should not be held for longer than 30 seconds, since doing so may harm the horse, even to the extent of causing permanent physical damage. Physical damage may take the following forms:

1. The nuchal ligament may be stressed beyond its limit and become severely painful or even tear, causing difficulty in grazing and drinking and staying in the round 'on the bit' position.
2. Muscle strain and resultant spasm may cause pain in the neck and back.
3. Too much pressure may be placed on the intervertebral discs and ligaments and lead to pressure on the nerve roots.
4. In a young horse, it can cause wobbler syndrome.
5. When this position is maintained for too long, the blood vessels in the neck can become constricted, leading to loss of circulation.

Psychologically, riding in this way places the rider in a position of total domination and the horse in a position of total, excessive, submission. All of the horse's natural defences are removed: with his nose so close to his body, he can only smell himself, and his vision is impaired to the extent that he can see only his own body, the ground, the sky, and some glimpses of the world in a more or less 'upside down' perspective.

While there may be those who see some advantage in such total subjugation, the ethical view is, surely, that we should show greater respect for the horse who is our partner in sport and in leisure. Nowadays, almost all riding is done in the name of sport and not through necessity. We should, therefore, seek to engender a genuine willingness on our horses' part to comply with our requirements, rather than enforcing our dominance upon them.

If we consider that the benefits claimed by practitioners of this method can be gained, without the attendant risks, by riding low and round, we can dismiss the extreme practice of deep and round as being unethical, unnecessary and probably counter-productive. The highly analytical trainer, Paul Belasik, has the following comment on this method:

I have found no logical, positive physical explanation for this new type of work. Horses trained in this system often exhibit a similar flaw of being unable to sink sufficiently in the haunches in highest collection – piaffe, for example. What seems, at first, to be roundness, turns into a lock, which seizes the lumbo-sacral area and prevents a coiling under of the pelvis.

Paul Belasik *Dressage for the 21st Century*

Relevant muscles and their functions

The head extensor muscles:
Splenius capitis
Longissimus capitis et atlantis
Semispinalis capitis (complexus)
Oblique capitis cranialis
These all act to lift the head.

The neck extensors:

Splenius cervicis extends the top two-thirds of the neck.

Semispinalis capitis extends the entire neck.

Spinalis cervicis extends the lower two-thirds of the neck.

Multifidus cervicis stabilizes the joints and is a weak extensor of the entire neck.

Longissimus cervicis extends the entire neck.

Trapezius extends the entire neck and forms a little hollow area in front of the wither when in action.

The rhomboids extend the entire neck.

Serratus cervicis extends the lower part of the neck when the forelimbs are fixed.

Figure 14. The neck extensors to be stretched: (a) below shows the superficial muscles and (b) over page the deep muscles.

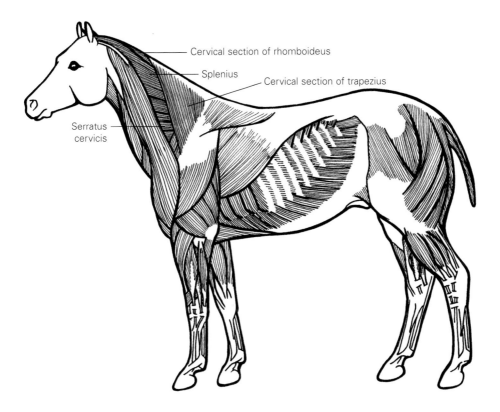

Cervical section of rhomboideus

Splenius

Cervical section of trapezius

Serratus cervicis

Figure 14(b) the deep muscles.

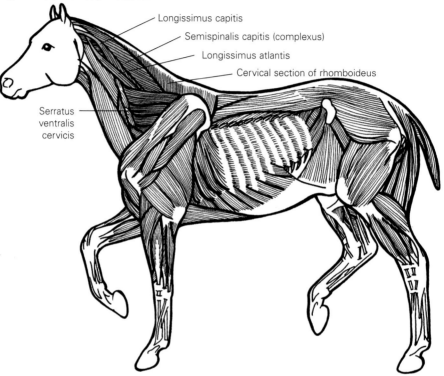

Longissimus capitis

Semispinalis capitis (complexus)

Longissimus atlantis

Cervical section of rhomboideus

Serratus ventralis cervicis

The neck should be stretched downwards to encourage roundness, to arch the back and to help extend the foreleg and thus stretch the triceps muscle. The sternocephalic and brachiocephalic muscles will contract in active downward and lateral stretching. When the horse stays down and is light in hand he will be stretching the top line extensors. If he is pulling against you he is contracting, and not stretching, his neck extensors.

Active Stretch Exercises for the Neck Extensors

The neck extensors are only stretched by means of active stretch exercises in the forward and low frame. To stretch the horse's neck down passively is almost impossible. The horse grazes with his neck extensors stretched, but pushing the head and neck down and keeping it there has little value. The only passive stretching of the extensors will be when they are stretched unilaterally sideways. This will be discussed in the section on lateral stretching (page 63 onwards). Active stretch exercises can be carried out as follows.

1. Feed the horse's hay on the stable floor. This is also a more natural and safer way to feed a horse than from a hanging hay-net.

2. Another dismounted exercise is to use a carrot or other titbit to coax the horse to stretch his neck down. This should motivate him to follow your hand. Place your hand so as to position him to perform the required stretch. Start at his nose and move the carrot downwards. You can stretch any relevant group of muscles by positioning your carrot higher, lower, closer to, or further from his body. You can put your hand between his forelegs for quite a strong top line stretch, or close to the ground, but further forward for a lighter stretch. Try to hold each position for 5–15 seconds, but if he can only maintain the stretch for 8 seconds, the muscles will still have stretched sufficiently.

The carrot stretch.

Riding long and low.

3. Ride low and round on a fairly loose rein. Ask the horse to stretch down, then yield with the reins. Eventually the horse will take the reins forward and stay there without you continually asking. Initially, however, you will have to explain to the horse, with take and give of the reins, that the requirement is to stay down (see *Successful Schooling*, page 42.) The further down the neck can

stretch, the more the extensor muscles will be stretched and the more the thoracic spine will flex. This posture will allow a fully lengthened position of the nuchal ligament and the supraspinous ligament, adding to the stability of the spine in this position. Try to facilitate a stretch to within a few inches from the ground. Start at walk and, once the horse can master this, proceed to the trot maintaining this position. Finally, do it in canter as well and maintain it through the transitions. Start with only a minute or two and slowly work up to approximately 5 minutes, allowing the horse freedom to place his neck where he feels comfortable. However, do not do this exercise for too long at a time as it can cause discomfort. Also, note that young horses should not be stretched down and round in too deep a frame as this may lead to hypermobility of the nuchal ligament, which can destabilize the vertebral column and cause strain and pain in the back muscles.

4. Walk over ground poles or cavalletti while asking the horse to stretch his neck down over the poles. The walk distance for ground poles is 2 ft 9 in – 3 ft 6 in (0.80 – 1.1m).

The neck stretching down over ground poles.

5. Trot over ground poles or cavalletti while asking the horse to stretch his neck down over the poles. The trot distance for ground poles is 3 ft 10 in – 5 ft (1.2 – 1.5m).

6. Ride low and round, but allow the horse to curl his neck round a little. This will give more stretch to the top line. This exercise is only necessary for horses with really tight nuchal ligaments and top line muscles and should be done gradually. Riding with his head too deep can cause problems, especially in a young horse.

Allowing the horse to curl his neck round (see exercise 6 in text).

7. Jump small obstacles and allow the horse to stretch his neck in a bascule – forwards and round.

8. Do gymnastic jumping grid exercises with the neck free to stretch forwards and round. Cross-poles are preferable to plain uprights as they encourage the horse to bascule and stretch his neck.

Bascule of neck and back over a small fence.

Stretching the Neck Flexors – Upward Stretch

The neck flexors should never be stretched actively by asking the horse to hollow his neck. This neck position initiates hollowness of the back and thus has a weakening effect on it. It also takes the horse off the bit and may affect the elasticity of the nuchal ligament and neck extensors, making riding on the bit more difficult. The neck flexors should only be stretched actively in the long and low position with the head stretched forwards. They should, however be stretched unilaterally, as tight flexor muscles can be a problem when bending sideways. This is because, in addition to flexing the neck longitudinally, the neck flexors also contract unilaterally to produce lateral flexion.

Passive stretching of the neck flexors should be done by a physiotherapist only, when the horse needs it for treatment of a specific condition.

Relevant muscles and their functions

Scalenus flexes the base of the neck.

Longus capitis flexes the top two-thirds of the neck as well as the head.

Longus colli flexes the entire neck.

Rectus capitis ventralis flexes the head onto the neck in the 'on the bit' position.

The neck muscles below the cervical spine will flex the neck when they contract bilaterally.

Figure 15. The neck flexors to be stretched.

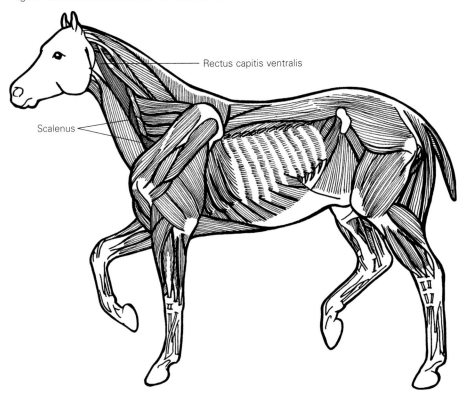

Active Stretch Exercises for the Neck Flexors

1. Feed the horse his hay off the ground. The horse will still be contracting his lower neck flexors, but he will be stretching his upper neck and head flexors.

2. While the horse is standing in the stable, hold a carrot or other titbit in front of

him so that he will stretch his neck and head forwards as far as it can go. This will lead to a slightly upward stretch without hollowing the back. Try to maintain the stretch for 5-15 seconds.

3. Mounted, ask the horse to stretch down, but instead of curling his neck round, ask him to stretch it down and forwards so that his head and neck are in a continuous line with very little flexion at the poll. This is achieved by asking with a take and give action on the reins, then allowing the reins to slip longer until the head is in full forward stretch and the reins are loose. This procedure is explained fully in *Successful Schooling*.

The neck stretching forward, following the carrot.

Stretching the Lateral Neck Flexors and Extensors – Sideways Stretch

Lateral stretching involves both the neck flexors and extensors. They are stretched unilaterally. Lateral flexion is greater in the top and lower parts of the neck than in the middle section. Young horses are naturally more supple, and find it easier to stretch laterally, than older horses who have already become set in their necks. Maintaining this suppleness in the young horse will lead to greater flexibility later on. Therefore mild lateral work should start early in training. These lateral stretch exercises will have a profound effect on a crooked horse. If the neck is not equally supple on both sides, the horse will not become straight. These exercises, together with lateral stretch exercises of the trunk, can straighten a horse in a relatively short time.

Relevant muscles and their functions

While the muscles are divided here into top, middle and lower neck groups for easier identification, note that the neck works as a unit because the muscles overlap. Thus isolated flexion of separate parts of the neck does not occur. Lateral flexion occurs when the neck flexor and extensor muscles contract unilaterally.

Upper part of the neck and the head
The sternocephalic inclines the head and bends it laterally.
Cleido-mastoideus, part of the brachiocephalic muscle, bends the head and neck laterally.
Longus capitis laterally flexes and rotates the top part of the neck as well as the head.
Oblique capitis cranialis flexes the head laterally.
Rectus capitis ventralis bends the head laterally.

Middle part of the neck
Multifidus cervicis rotates the neck.
Omotransversarius flexes the 2nd to the 4th vertebrae laterally.
Intertransversarii cervicis flex the entire neck laterally.
Splenius bends the top two-thirds of the neck laterally.
Semispinalis capitis (complexus) bends the entire neck laterally.

Lower part of the neck
Longus colli flexes the entire neck laterally from the 3rd cervical vertebra.
Sternocephalicus bends the neck laterally.
Scalenus bends the lower half (base of the neck) laterally.
Longissimus cervicis bends the head and the entire neck laterally.
Multifidus cervicis bends the entire neck laterally.
Intertransversarii bend the entire neck laterally.
Serratus ventralis cervicis bends the lower part of the neck laterally in unilateral contraction.
Brachiocephalicus bends the entire neck laterally.

Figure 16. The lateral neck flexors to be stretched: (a) shows the superficial muscles and (b) the deep muscles.

(a)

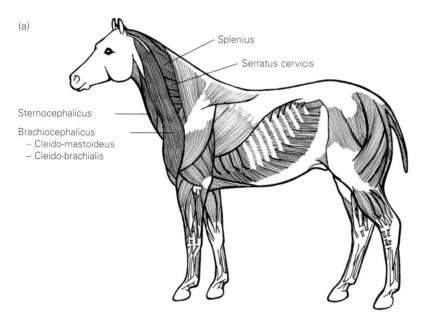

Splenius

Serratus cervicis

Sternocephalicus

Brachiocephalicus
 – Cleido-mastoideus
 – Cleido-brachialis

(b)

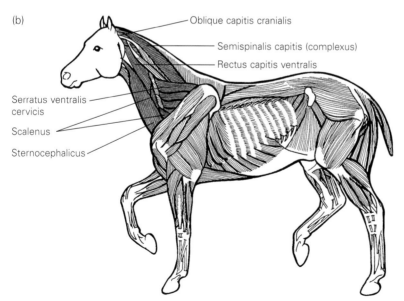

Oblique capitis cranialis

Semispinalis capitis (complexus)

Rectus capitis ventralis

Serratus ventralis cervicis

Scalenus

Sternocephalicus

Active Stretch Exercises for the Lateral Neck Flexors

1. Hang the hay-net outside to the side of the horse's stable. He will then have to turn his head and neck to reach it.

2. Use a carrot (or other titbit) and move it towards the side of the horse's body. He will flex his neck to reach it. You can place the carrot higher, lower, further back or only slightly to the side to effect the necessary amount of stretch. Tease him a little by holding it slightly out of reach if you need a longer hold on the stretch. The horse is quite capable of scratching his rump with his teeth when he is itchy. However, although he can stretch that far, he should not touch his hip or belly with his nose as, to do so, he might rotate his shoulder and lose the stretch. If you ask him to stretch too far, your horse will straighten out by moving his hindquarters the other way to relieve the discomfort. This would be a clear example of a righting reaction where the spine is brought into alignment with the head. You have to inhibit this automatic reaction to procure the full stretch. Do all the movements slowly to inhibit this righting reaction. Note that these stretches should be done bilaterally. Try to maintain them for 5–15 seconds.

3. Mounted, at the halt, ask the horse to move his nose down and sideways, then release the rein pressure. As soon as, or even before, he starts to move his nose forward (if you have good sensitivity you will feel seconds before he actually lifts his head), ask him to stretch down and sideways again. The important part of this exercise is that the horse uses his inside neck flexors to bend his neck. This means that the outside muscles will be relaxed and able to stretch. Should there be weight in your inside hand, this could mean that the horse is still contracting his outside neck muscles and therefore they cannot stretch. Or it could mean that he has put too much weight onto his inside foreleg (falling-in on the shoulder) and is using his outside neck muscles in an attempt to maintain his balance.

4. Also at the halt, push with your inside leg against the girth and ask the horse to bend his neck towards your toe. Do not try to force the bend, or the righting reaction will set in and the horse will keep his back straight and move his hind

legs sideways, away from the stretch, instead of bending his neck. When he is not yielding to the rein his hind legs will spin, in a circle, around his forelegs. Convince him to bend his neck with take and give (see *Successful Schooling*, page 42).

5. Ride the horse in the low and round frame, but ask for inside lateral bend at the same time.

Asking for inside lateral bend while riding low and round.

This exercise can be performed at the walk, trot or canter. You may ask the horse to bend sideways as far as is needed, but it is imperative that he uses his own muscles and that you do not hang onto the inside rein (should this happen, the stretch will become passive and this can cause muscle injury). Use a light-handed approach of take and give. The rider should always ride with a yielding hand. As the late Dr Reiner Klimke said, 'make the horse an offer' (give the reins).

The lateral bend should not be maintained for longer than 30 seconds. Beware of the 'false bend'. This effect can be observed when the rider pulls the horse's head to the inside, with the inside hand. To the onlooker, this may appear to be an inside bend, but the inside neck flexors are not contracting. The inside rein has a strong contact and the outside rein has no contact. In effect, the horse is pulling on the rider's inside hand with his outside neck flexors. Although these muscles may well be in a long frame they are, in fact, contracting. Therefore, there will be no stretch in them.

6. Add counter-flexion to the above exercise. Alternate inside bend and counter-bending slowly at the walk, trot and canter a few strides at a time. Start on the long side of the arena and, for a stronger stretching effect, do it on the circle. Make sure that there is no resistance to the counter-bend, or it will have no effect. The horse's head should never be pulled from side to side; this would be counter-productive. He should yield to the rider's hand for both bend and counter-bend. If you should feel a pull or 'hold' on the rein, the horse is using the incorrect muscles, which will lead to no stretch at all. Use the 'take and give' method as described in *Successful Schooling* to achieve the correct effect. Over-emphasize the bend for a stronger stretching effect.

   We do the counter-flexion exercise for two reasons. One of the principles of proprioceptive-neuro-muscular facilitation is that 'maximum contraction will lead to maximum relaxation'. Therefore, maximum contraction in counter-flexion will lead to maximum relaxation of those muscles with the resultant easier bend to the inside. The other effect counter-flexion has is to elicit a stretch reflex in the muscles on the opposite side of the neck. This will make them contract and the outside neck flexors will relax automatically.

7. Do the same exercises in the normal 'on the bit' position and in a low, round frame to work the different muscles groups.

8. Ride serpentines. Start with 20 m loops and progress to smaller loops. When the loops become smaller use backtracking for a stronger suppling effect. For a really pleasant exercise try to fit as many loops into the manège as you can. Aim for about 16 and try to improve your record on that.

9. Ride circles, in trot, at every marker. Start with 20 m circles at the appropriate markers and work down to 8 m circles. Decrease the size of the circles

Figure 17. Illustrations of two effects of counter-flexion. (a) Maximum contraction of the left side neck flexors will lead to maximum relaxation of those same muscles, with the resultant easier bend to the right. (b) The stretch reflex. When the horse's left side neck flexors contract, those on the right side are stretched. The resultant stretch reflex will lead to contraction of the right side neck flexors, thus improving the inside bend.

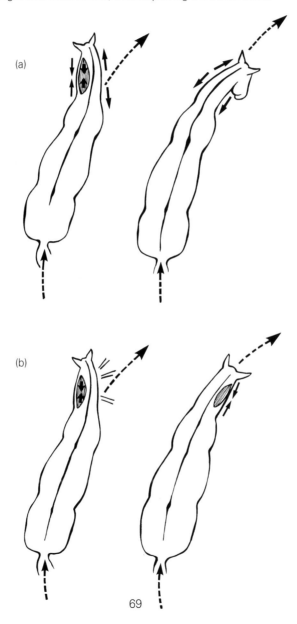

Exercises in counter-flexion.

according to the horse's level of suppleness. Small circles will necessarily be ridden at a slower pace than the large circles. Suppleness should still be maintained once the horse is supple enough to perform the small circles.

10. Ride a serpentine, but put in a circle on every loop. Increase the stretch by making smaller loops, with smaller circles on each loop.

11. Ride a tiny serpentine up the centre line (5 m each side of the centre line). This teaches the horse to keep his neck relaxed and ready for quick changes of bend. He learns to react (yield) immediately to a light squeeze of the reins.

12. Ride figures of eight, starting with two large circles and, as the horse becomes more supple, slowly decreasing the size of the circles down to 6 m. The smaller

the circle, the slower and shorter the trot stride has to be in order to maintain balance. Throughout these exercises the horse has to yield completely to light rein aids, otherwise his hindquarters will swing out. Once the horse can master 6 m circles correctly, he has reached a sufficient level of suppleness. He will only maintain the suppleness, however, by doing stretch exercises throughout his career.

13. Ride a spiral and change the rein from the small circle onto a 20 m circle on the other rein. This is a very comfortable change, which the horses seem to enjoy. Keep the neck very supple as the circle becomes smaller. If the horse becomes hard against your inside hand, he will be contracting his outside neck muscles instead of stretching them. The righting reaction will come into play which will make his hindquarters swing out. If you prevent him from tightening his neck muscles and he continues to yield to your hands, he will be able to step into the tracks of his forelegs and he will be straight. When appropriate, decrease the figure down to 6 m.

14. Ride a flat figure of eight on the long side of the manège. Ride a 12 or 10 m half-circle at S and return to the track at E. Change the bend and diagonal as soon as the half-circle is complete and push the horse back to the track. Ride on the track with the new inside bend up to V. At V do a 12 m or 10 m half-circle and return to E, with a definite change to the new bend and diagonal well before E while pushing the horse back to the track. Repeat a number of times, decreasing the size of the half- circles for a stronger stretch and suppling effect.

15. Ride counter-canter with a few strides of counter-flexion of the neck. This gives a good lateral neck stretch, especially for the lower part of the neck. Start by doing this around the entire arena, then on a 20 m circle. Establish good balance and make sure that the horse is light in hand and balancing himself, then slowly ask for a few strides of outside bend. Slowly alternate the inside and outside bend. If the horse goes hard in your hands, he has lost balance and will more than likely do a flying change or break the canter. This exercise helps the horse to improve his balance and prevents him from setting his neck in the counter-canter. When the horse has learnt to balance in both flexion and counter-flexion, he will be less likely to break the counter-canter or lose balance and fall into a flying change. The flying changes will also be more balanced.

Stretch Exercises for Your Horse

Figure 18. Some active stretch exercises for the lateral neck flexors:

(a) serpentine with circle in loop.

(b) tiny serpentine up the centre line.

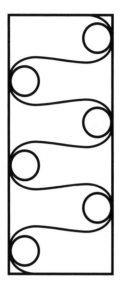

(c) figure of eight.

d) spiral: change of rein from the small inner circle onto a 20 m circle.

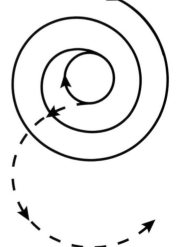

Figure 19. The flat figure of eight.

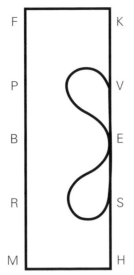

Counter-canter, alternating inside and outside bend of the neck, is an exercise that prevents the horse from setting his neck and helps to improve his balance.

Passive Stretch Exercises for the Lateral Neck Flexors

Most horses find it more difficult to stretch laterally to one side than to the other. These horses will feel, to the rider, as though they 'won't take hold' of the bit on one side, whereas on the other side, they will feel as though they are 'holding on' to the bit and pulling the rider's arm. This phenomenon has actually nothing to do with the mouth at all, but is a product of the natural crookedness that is inherent, to some extent, in all horses. This crookedness is apparent in the horse's ability to yield more readily to the rider's hand on one side than on the other. For the sake of clarity, we can call the easy side the concave side and the difficult side the convex side – although significant degrees of concavity and convexity may no longer be apparent in horses who have received correct training. The basic cause of the differential feel in the rein contact lies in the difficulty the horse has in stretching the muscles on his concave side The muscles on this side are shortened and thus less supple. Therefore, when the horse is being ridden towards his opposite (convex) side, these muscles cannot stretch adequately and the horse will feel as though he is 'holding onto the bit' on the inside rein. Because of this, he will lack the inside bend and consequently stays too light on the outside rein. This is evident, to some extent, in all movements, but is particularly obvious in turns and circles towards the convex side. To rectify this, simply dismount once you have warmed up your horse's muscles, and do one or two passive lateral neck stretches towards the difficult side, as described below. These passive neck stretches are very rewarding and, when you mount again, you will find that the horse will immediately yield more readily to the rein contact on the 'hard' side.

The horse's position during these exercises is important, in order to ensure that the correct muscles are stretched. He should stand with his feet square and his shoulders level.

Three methods for the lateral neck stretch
Method one
Stretching the near side. Stand at your horse's side, facing his neck. Place your right hand against the vertebral column with an open palm. Find a vertebra by palpating the middle of the brachiocephalic muscle. The hard bump you will find is the 5th cervical vertebra. You will find that it is closer to the lower border of the neck than you would have expected. You can place your hand on any vertebra, depend-

ing where you want the most stretch. The middle part of the neck has the least natural stretch and probably needs the most passive stretching. The left hand holds the halter or bridle below the horse's ear. This will bend his neck, rather than bending his head onto the neck. Pull very slowly on the halter/bridle while pushing lightly on the vertebra. It is important to maintain even pressure on the vertebra. When you feel resistance, hold for a few seconds then yield slightly by relaxing, then slowly stretch a little more and hold for 5–15 seconds. Should the horse show resistance to this stretch, hold it where he is comfortable, move it back to its normal position and try again the next day. You will see a marked improvement to this stretch each day. You should be able to stretch most of the neck muscles by positioning the neck higher or lower, by placing your hand higher up the neck towards his head or lower down, and by turning his nose towards or away from you with your left hand holding the noseband.

You can do this exercise during your schooling session. When your horse finds it difficult to yield to your hand on one side, you may dismount and stretch his neck to the difficult side with the above method. When you mount again and ride circles to that side, you will notice an immediate and marked improvement in his ability to yield to the 'hard' side. The nineteenth century French trainer, François Baucher, did these stretches before mounting and called them 'flexions'. Although he may not have thought of this work in today's terms, he was practising passive stretching during the mid-nineteenth century!

Method two
If you find the method of holding your hand over the vertebra difficult, you may put your hand over the horse's mane with your forearm perpendicular to the ground and press against his vertebra with the lower part of your forearm. Your other hand will pull on the halter, the cheekpiece of the bridle, or over the horse's nose. You can work your way up or down the neck in this manner, wherever the most stretch is needed.

Method three
Stand beside your horse's neck and face forwards. Place the palm of your left hand over his cheek while your other hand goes under his throat and over his nose bone. Curl his neck around you as you turn. Maintain the vertical position of the head to ensure that the correct muscles are stretched.

Photos to show the three methods of the lateral neck stretch. (a) Method one.

(b) Method two.

(c) Method three.

Stretch Exercises for Your Horse

The head-on-neck stretch.

Head-on-neck stretch

Horses often twist or tilt their heads slightly while doing lateral work such as shoulder-in or half-pass. This usually happens only on one side, while the 'good' side will bend uniformly. The horse will evade bending the top part of his neck by turning the tip of his nose slightly to the outside while his neck is bent to the inside. Alternatively, he may rotate his head so that the nose points to the inside, but the top part of the neck does not bend at all. To the rider, it will feel as though the horse does not want to 'take the rein' on that side. This however, has nothing to do with 'taking the rein', but is all about tightness in the muscles which run from his head to the top part of his neck. This inability to stretch is usually only on the one side.

The problem can be rectified by bending his head onto his neck. Stand at the horse's near side, facing his head and neck. Hold the horse's nose by placing your left hand over it or by holding the noseband. Place your right hand over his cheek, with the heel of your hand on the lower border of his cheek. Push the cheek while pulling the noseband to acquire the bend. Keep the pressure on the cheek in a downward direction. Prevent the head from rotating at the poll to ensure that the correct muscles are stretched. This will stretch the longus capitis, obliquus capitis cranialis, rectus capitis ventralis, longissimus capitis and cleido-mastoideus. A significant difference will be noted after only a few days of stretching.

The Back and Trunk

Since the back forms the foundation against which the limbs move, any stiffness in the back will have an adverse effect on movement. Only if the back is supple will optimum movement be possible. Racehorses, jumpers, eventers and dressage horses are often out of action as a consequence of back pain. Preventing such pain is therefore very important.

Stretching the Trunk and Loin Extensors – Arching the Back

It is essential for all equine athletes to maintain suppleness in the back and loins. By contracting the abdominal muscles, the back will stretch. The abdominal muscles (rectus abdominis, internal and external abdominal oblique) as well as the hip flexors (iliopsoas) are responsible for lumbo-sacral and hip flexion.

When these muscles contract, the bottom line is shortened while the top line is lengthened. Thus the hindquarters become more engaged, increasing the amplitude of movement, the horse becomes more comfortable to ride and the weight-bearing capacity is improved. Most of the flexion and extension of the back occurs in the lumbo-sacral and cervico-thoracic junctures. The other joints have very little capacity to flex and extend. Lowering the neck will automatically involve flexion and arching of the thoracic section of the back. This slight flexion is caused by the traction exerted by the nuchal ligament on the spinous processes of the first thoracic vertebrae and by the automatic righting and balancing reactions of the horse, which will automatically produce contraction of the abdominal muscles.

The lumbo-sacral joint is very important, as keeping it supple will help to create engagement and to develop power, and will thus improve athletic ability, lengthening of the stride and jumping ability. This joint is important for the maintenance of balance, as the hind limbs are crucial for regaining balance.

Relevant muscles and their functions

Trunk extensors
Spinalis thoracis extends the thoracic vertebrae.
Longissimus thoracis extends the vertebral column.
Iliocostalis thoracis extends the vertebral column.
Multifidus thoracis and lumborum twist the vertebral column.
Serratus dorsalis caudalis extends the thoracic vertebrae.

Loin extensors
Medial gluteus extends and abducts the hip, but with its connection to longissimus lumborum extends the loins.
Accessory gluteus assists the medial gluteus.
Longissimus lumborum extends the lumbar spine as well as the hip through its connection to the medial gluteus muscle.

All these muscles are interconnected from the croup to the poll. Contraction of the abdominal muscles will lead to stretching of the entire group of extensors. The horse can only round and stretch his back when his back muscles are relaxed.

Figure 20. The trunk and loin extensors to be stretched: (a) shows the superficial muscles and (b) the deep muscles.

(a)

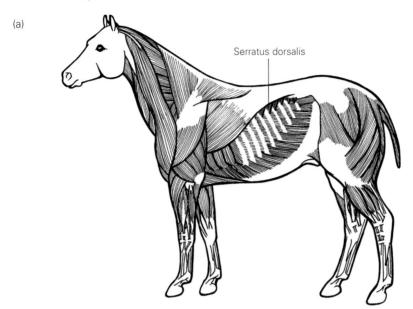

Serratus dorsalis

(b)

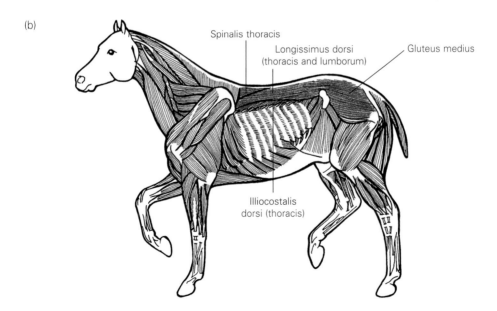

Spinalis thoracis

Longissimus dorsi
(thoracis and lumborum)

Gluteus medius

Illiocostalis
dorsi (thoracis)

Exercises to prepare the horse's back for carrying the rider

1. Elicit a few hip flexion reflexes by drawing two lines on either side of the horse's rump. See Passive Stretch Exercises for the Back and Loin Extensors – Hip flexion reflex (pages 88–9) for a full description.

2. Elicit a few abdominal flexion reflexes by pressing your fingertips into the abdomen. See Passive Stretch Exercises for the Back and Loin Extensors – Abdominal reflex (page 88) for a full description.

3. Ask the horse to stretch his head down to his toes with the help of a carrot.

4. Stretch his head and neck to either side with the help of a carrot.

5. Walking in-hand for two to three minutes up and down an incline and around the handler will help to mobilize the vertebrae by stretching the deep muscles and ligaments around the joints. It will promote circulation and, through the stimulation of the Golgi cells, will improve body awareness (proprioception) and promote a faster response and adaptation to the rider's weight.

Active Stretch Exercises for the Trunk and Loin Extensors

In order to stretch the loins actively the iliopsoas (iliacus and psoas major) and the abdominal muscles have to contract. During the contraction of these muscles the back becomes rounded, the loin flexes and the hindquarters are drawn under the body.

1. Feed the horse his hay off the floor. The downward stretch of the neck will lead to arching of the back.

2. Riding low and round in trot and canter stretches the powerful longissimus muscles and the juxta-vertebral muscles. It strengthens the rectus abdominis and abdominal oblique as well as psoas and iliacus (iliopsoas). It renders the spine more supple and mobile and makes the horse more comfortable to ride. Ride transitions walk-trot-canter and canter-trot-walk while maintaining this frame. Riding low and round should not be done for too long periods at a time.

The horse should dictate the length of time in order to protect his tiring muscles. Maintaining this frame improves the horse's ability to engage his hindquarters as it makes the lumbo-sacral joint more supple. The horse is 'compelled', by his automatic balance reactions, to bring his hindquarters more underneath him in order to maintain his balance and not put weight on his forehand.

Low and round in canter.

3. Walk and trot over 6–8 ground poles and small cavalletti, encouraging the horse to stretch his head and neck down. Keep the first and last poles spaced a little closer than the middle poles. If the distance of the first two poles is too long and you do not bring the horse close enough to the first pole, he will take an extra step in the first or second space. If all the poles are of an equal distance and the distance is too long, he will take an extra step in the last space. By putting extra steps in, he will thus shorten his stride instead of lengthening it.

Figure 21. Spacing ground poles: note that the first and last poles are placed at slightly shorter distances than the rest (see text).

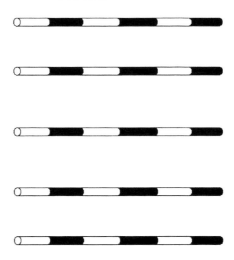

4. Longeing exercises for stretching should be performed for only 5 minutes on each rein at the trot. For the purpose of stretching one should use a chambon, German side reins or two reins (long reining). Fixed side reins do not allow the horse enough freedom to stretch down. Trot over poles or cavalletti at a slow tempo, but maintain the cadence. This helps to free the movement and to loosen the spine. It activates the abdominal muscles to contract, and thus stretches the top line muscles. The horse should be encouraged to stretch down.

5. Do gymnastic jumping with small cross-poles. Allow with the hands to encourage a good bascule. This bascule is important to produce the required stretch.

6. Perform rein-back exercises. Start with a few steps only, then slowly build up to 6–8 steps. Rein-back up a slight incline for a few metres. This exercise has a very strong stretching effect on the loin extensors, therefore you should start with only one or two steps then increase the amount slowly. Do not repeat this exercise too many times as it may cause muscle strain. The rein-back is physically difficult for the horse, since he has to lift his hind legs one at a time without putting his weight on his forehand. This means that the one hind leg has to carry the horse's weight while the other is moving backwards and vice versa.

Longeing with German side reins.

Rein-back up a small incline. Note hip flexion and stretch in the loins.

His natural inclination would be to put his weight on his forehand, lift his head, and then step backward with a hollow back.

7. All transitions strengthen the abdominal muscles and the iliopsoas and therefore stretch the loin muscles. Start with trot-walk-trot transitions and progress to trot-halt-trot transitions. To perform these correctly the horse will have to bring his hindquarters more underneath him.

8. Do canter-trot-canter transitions and when the horse can master this with balance and ease, do canter-walk-canter transitions. The latter exercise develops the most power in the bottom line muscles and stretch in the top line. If the horse is allowed to dive down in this transition, there will be no stretch in the loin area. Transitions within the gait, collection to extension, also help to stretch and supple the loins.

9. Working in all gaits up and down slopes and hills has a good suppling effect on the loins. The canter uphill obviously has the most stretching effect on these muscles.

10. Canter and extended canter normally involve more lumbar flexion thus more stretch than the other gaits.

11. The loins flex most at the gallop and during transitions. The abdominal muscles and iliopsoas flex the loins at each stride of the gallop. This explains why racehorses have strong abdominal muscles with the resultant lean, flat belly. Gallop should, however not be attempted early in training as strain injuries may occur and undue stress may also be placed upon the heart and lungs.

Passive Stretch Exercises for the Trunk and Loin Extensors
Tail stretch

This stretches the entire spine of the horse. Horses seem to enjoy this stretch. It produces a feeling of deep relaxation and as such is an excellent way of ending the stretching session. Horses tend to stretch their trunk and neck away from the tail stretch, thereby creating traction to the entire vertebral column.

While standing next to the horse, stroke over his gluteal muscles toward the tail, keep your left hand on the seat bone and lift the tail slowly with the other hand a few centimetres from the base of the tail. If the horse pinches (clamps) his tail, use both hands, one on top and the other underneath, to pick it up. (The stretch is only possible once the horse has relaxed his tail.) Move to a position behind him and rotate the tail slowly a few times in both directions to loosen it. This will release the reflexive clamping-down of the tail when it is touched. Then, with both hands around the tail, use your body weight to pull the tail back very gently. Hold the stretch for one or two minutes unless the horse shows discomfort. At this point the horse may start to pull against you. This will give an even better stretch. Release the stretch progressively to allow the horse to adjust, then replace the tail.

CAUTION: Should the horse's tail feel loose and give to the stretch, he may have pathology in his joints. Consult your veterinarian.

The tail stretch – note how the horse stretches forwards against the pull.

Abdominal reflex

Although this is not technically a passive exercise, it fits into this category of stretches. It is a reflex stretch and it elicits an automatic reaction of abdominal contraction and the subsequent stretching of the back. Use your fingertips, with your hand in a claw shape, to press upward, under the abdomen. Do not use your nails. Use sharp prods with your fingertips to elicit a quick contraction of the abdominal muscles. Alternatively, press with your thumb at the end of the sternum or slide both hands underneath the horse's abdomen and lift his trunk up slowly. CAUTION: Some horses may kick out at this prodding.

The abdominal reflex exercise. Compare the shape of the horse's back to the shape in the lower photo on p. 76. This is the same horse.

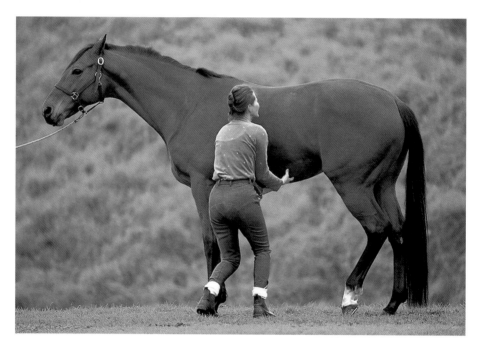

Hip flexion reflex

Stroke the horse along his back as you walk to stand behind him. Place both hands flat on his rump on both sides, slightly behind the croup. Then, with the point of your thumbs, draw a 20 cm line each side of the croup roughly 7 cm from the spine and parallel to it, from top to tail. Press fairly hard, but not so hard that it would hurt the horse. The horse should react by contracting his abdominal muscles, flexing his loins and arching his back. If the horse does not react, you are probably not pressing hard enough.

Hip flexion reflex. Note the almost dramatic rounding of the loins and tilting of the pelvis.

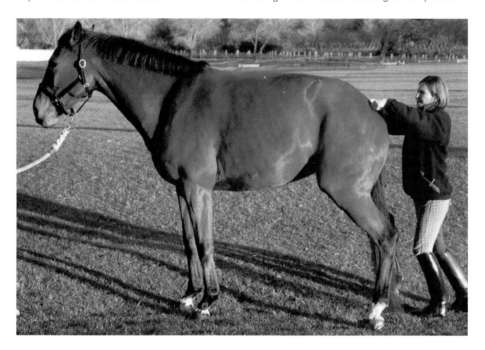

Stretching the Trunk and Loin Flexors
The trunk flexors are the abdominal muscles and these do not usually need stretching as it can lead to back weakness. In very specific cases, usually resulting from injury, they may need to be worked on by a trained equine physiotherapist.

Relevant muscles and their functions
Psoas minor flexes the pelvis on the loins and produces lateral inclination of the pelvis and flexion of the lumbo-sacral and sacroiliac joints.
Rectus abdominis flexes the lumbar spine and the lumbo-sacral joint.
Transverse abdominis effects trunk flexion when contracting bilaterally.

Internal and external abdominal oblique muscles effect trunk flexion during bilateral contraction.

The horse will stretch these muscles when attempting to clear an obstacle with his hind legs when jumping. He will even twist his trunk to get them out of the way of the obstacle. During this excessive twist he can strain a muscle and injure it.

Stretching the Lateral Flexors of the Trunk

The vertebral column in the trunk area, by way of its anatomy, does not allow much lateral bend. The attachment of the ribs in the thoracic area prevents lateral bend and in the lumbar area the angles of the facets also limit lateral bend. Stretching is brought about by the muscles moving the ribcage over to one side which, in the ridden horse, is usually in response to a push or signal from the rider's leg. The more mobile the ribcage, the more the muscles in between will stretch.

Relevant muscles and their functions

Unilateral contraction of the extensors and flexors of the spine will lead to lateral stretch of the twin muscles on the other side.

Internal and external abdominal oblique muscles support the abdominal viscera. When contracting unilaterally they assist with lateral flexion.

The transverse abdominal muscle flexes the trunk laterally when contracting unilaterally.

The internal and external intercostal muscles are primarily breathing-muscles, but they bring the ribs closer together, which enables the ribcage to move over when they contract unilaterally.

The iliocostalis thoracis stabilize the lumbar vertebrae and ribs. They extend the vertebral column and, when contracting unilaterally, produce lateral flexion.

Multifidus thoracis and lumborum twist the vertebral column.

Intertransversarii stabilize the vertebral column and produce lateral bend when contracting unilaterally.

Longissimus dorsi helps with lateral flexion.

Figure 22. The trunk and loin flexors to be stretched: (a) shows the superficial muscles and (b) the deep muscles.

(a)

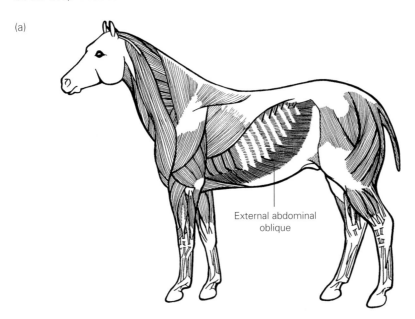

External abdominal
oblique

(b)

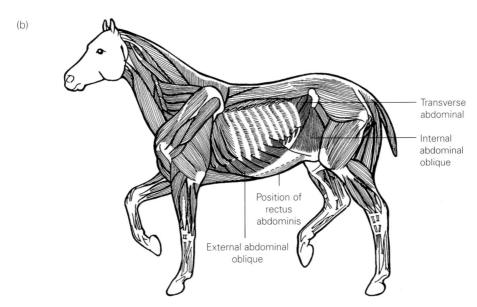

Transverse
abdominal

Internal
abdominal
oblique

Position of
rectus
abdominis

External abdominal
oblique

Figure 23. The lateral trunk flexors to be stretched: (a) shows the superficial muscles and (b) the deep muscles.

(a)

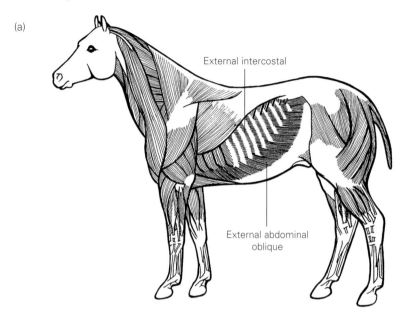

External intercostal

External abdominal oblique

(b)

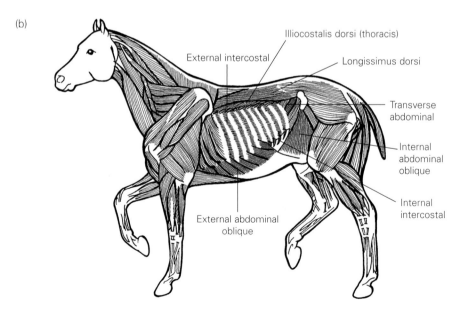

Illiocostalis dorsi (thoracis)

External intercostal

Longissimus dorsi

Transverse abdominal

Internal abdominal oblique

Internal intercostal

External abdominal oblique

Active Stretch Exercises for the Lateral Flexors of the Trunk

The lateral exercises of shoulder-in, travers, renvers and half-pass should be performed at the walk. At this gait the stretch is slow and more effective. It is also easier to maintain the bend. When the horse is doing lateral work at the trot or canter, the elevation and thrust in these gaits help to move the horse over. He can therefore evade the stretch, with the result that there is less stretch on the muscles.

The first five exercises are similar to the exercises for the lateral stretch of the neck. They are repeated here for ease of reference.

1. Use a carrot as motivation to encourage the horse to bend to the side. Move the carrot further back and away from the body to encourage him to stretch his abdominal muscles. Stand with your back against the horse so that he has to bend around you. Try to maintain these carrot stretches for 5–15 seconds.

Using a carrot to motivate lateral flexor stretch. Note the stretch on the outside of the neck.

2. Ride circles in trot and canter, starting with large circles, and work your way down to a volte. You can ride these circles at every appropriate marker, or every second marker Always start the circles at the trot to prepare the muscles. However, circles at the canter will produce better quality muscle fibre because the muscles have to stretch and stabilize the horse for balance simultaneously.

3. Ride serpentines at the trot with strong half-halts before the change of bend and a deep change of bend with backtracking in between the loops to emphasize the stretch. This will lead to quicker relaxation of the antagonists and more stretch, with a better suppling effect. Try to put as many loops as you can in the serpentine.

Figure 24. Backtracking the loops of a serpentine.

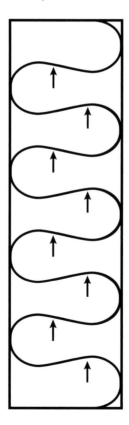

4. Ride a flat figure of eight on the long side of the manège. Ride a 12 m or 10 m half-circle at S and return to the track at E. Change the bend and diagonal as soon as the half-circle is complete and push the horse back to the track. Ride on the track with the new inside bend up to V. At V ride a 12 m or 10 m half-circle and return to E, with a definite change to the new bend and diagonal well before E while pushing the horse back to the track. Repeat a number of times, decreasing the size of the half-circles for a stronger stretch and suppling effect.

5. Ride spirals, reducing the size gradually to 6 m, then push the horse out again, or change the bend from the middle and ride another 20 m circle on the other rein (see Figure 18(d), page 72). It is most important to keep the neck very supple during this exercise, otherwise the righting reaction will come into play and this will stiffen the back and no stretching will be possible. If you keep the contact soft and yielding, the horse will step with his hind feet into the tracks of his forefeet and thus stretch the outside muscles. Spiralling in at the canter will have a stronger stretching effect on the muscles. Push the horse out in a leg-yield to maintain the stretch. Bring the horse out of the spiral before he breaks gait.

6. Ride shoulder-fore and shoulder-in. These exercises stretch the internal oblique muscle on the outside, while it contracts on the inside. This contraction helps to strengthen the vertebral column, thus preventing back problems. Long-backed horses should do shoulder-fore before starting the shoulder-in, as too much stretching could weaken the back. Do this work mainly at the walk to achieve the most stretch. Shoulder-in on the circle will encourage a stronger stretch.

7. Ride travers and renvers at the walk, aiming for an ever-deeper angle on a circle or around corners.

8. Ride half-pass at the walk. To get more stretch, increase the angle and push over more.

9. Counter-canter on a 20 m circle is an excellent exercise for stretching the abdominal oblique muscles, while the rectus abdominis and iliopsoas muscles have to work in a lengthened frame to keep the pelvic tilt without the help of the

Travers.

Renvers.

whole abdominal group of muscles. This is therefore an excellent stretching, straightening and strengthening exercise as the muscles are working in the outer range of movement. As a result of the simultaneous stretch and contraction, better quality muscle fibres with enhanced strength and elasticity develop, and fine motor control of the muscle is improved. Ensure that the horse maintains the lightness of the forehand. If he loses lightness he will lose balance and break the canter or do a flying change. Start by riding around the arena and progress to 20 m circles, then slowly decrease the size of the circle for a stronger stretch on the inside muscles. Ride a figure of eight, alternating true canter with counter-canter; the first circle in true canter and the second in

Counter-canter is a valuable exercise for the lateral flexors of the trunk.

counter-canter. Start with two 20 m circles and decrease the size at each attempt until you can ride two 10 m circles.

10. Ride shoulder-in through the transitions during canter, trot, and walk. Start with shoulder-in at the walk and go directly from walk shoulder-in to trot shoulder-in and back again to walk shoulder-in. Keep alternating, but do not lose the shoulder-in. Do the same with canter shoulder-in to walk shoulder-in. This is a very difficult exercise and needs experience and time to perfect. It is nevertheless an extremely good stretch exercise.

Passive Stretch Exercises for the Lateral Flexors of the Trunk

Stand at your horse's side behind his shoulder, facing his ribcage. Hold the rein or lead rein in one hand while your other hand, fingers pointing up, is on the horse's ribcage, more or less on the girth area. Push the ribcage over very slowly with your palm flat. If this is not effective you may have to use the backs of your fingers with your hand flexed at the knuckles. Hold for 5–15 seconds. Use the rein to prevent the horse from stepping forwards or sideways out of the pressure. Do not push too hard or too fast or you will disturb the horse's balance and he will then move out of the stretch. Push only as far as he will allow while he is happily standing still. This stretches the intercostal and abdominal oblique muscles.

The Forelimbs

Maintaining suppleness in the forelimbs is essential to the prevention of injury, especially for jumpers, eventers and racehorses.

Stretching the Forelimb Retractors – Forward Stretch

Stretching these muscles will help the horse to develop good extended gaits. It will lead to freer shoulder movement and thus enhance the dressage horse's natural gaits and it will help the jumper to lift his forelegs out of the way of the obstacle and protect his flexor tendons from strain injury during the landing. In racing, the horse stretches his limbs actively through large ranges of movement, combined with top speed. When weight and speed are combined, the strain on the separate front feet is increased, with the resultant tendency toward superficial digital flexor tendon injuries. The fetlock touches the ground at every stride and the stretch in the flexor muscles is enormous. Bowed tendons (superficial flexor tendon tears and strain injuries) are some of the most common injuries in racehorses. With stretch exercises, the racehorse should gain a longer stride and the foreleg tendons should become more flexible and more protected from strain injuries.

Passive stretching of the intercostal and abdominal oblique muscles. Note the ribcage pushing out on the horse's near side.

Figure 25. The forelimb retractors to be stretched: (a) shows the superficial muscles and (b) the deep muscles.

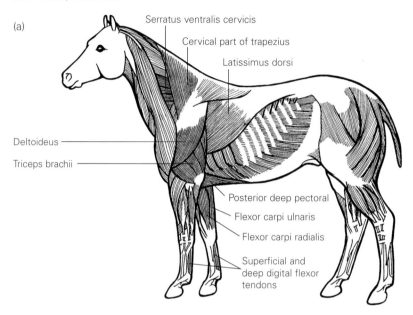

(a)

Serratus ventralis cervicis

Cervical part of trapezius

Latissimus dorsi

Deltoideus

Triceps brachii

Posterior deep pectoral

Flexor carpi ulnaris

Flexor carpi radialis

Superficial and deep digital flexor tendons

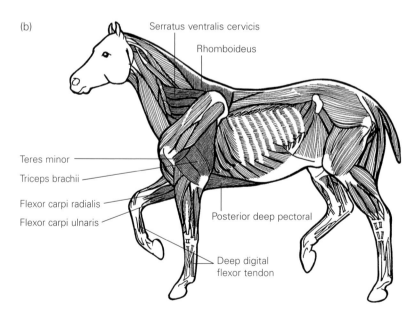

(b)

Serratus ventralis cervicis

Rhomboideus

Teres minor

Triceps brachii

Flexor carpi radialis

Flexor carpi ulnaris

Posterior deep pectoral

Deep digital flexor tendon

Relevant muscles and their functions

Cervical part of serratus ventralis pulls the top of the scapula forward.

Rhomboideus cervicalis and thoracalis stabilize the top of the scapula.

Cervical part of trapezius stabilizes the scapula.

Triceps brachii flexes the shoulder joint and extends the elbow joint.

Latissimus dorsi flexes the shoulder joint.

Posterior deep pectoral brings the upper limb backwards and inwards.

Teres minor flexes the shoulder joint.

Teres major flexes the shoulder joint.

Deltoideus flexes the shoulder joint.

Deep and superficial digital flexor muscles draw the forearm backwards and flex the knee, fetlock and digits of the foot and extend the elbow.

Flexor carpi radialis flexes the knee, fetlock and pastern joints.

Flexor carpi ulnaris flexes the knee.

Active Stretch Exercises for the Forelimb Retractors

1. Walk in a low and round frame. Use your seat to lengthen the walk – the leg aids often lead to a faster but shorter stride. When in this position, make sure that your horse does not pull on the reins. The contact must be light. If the horse pulls on the reins, he will be using his vertebral extensors to hollow his back and this will inhibit the freedom of his shoulders.

2. Trot in a low and round frame. The horse's stride is at its longest when the croup, shoulders and ears are at the same level. This frame releases the scapula forward-rotator muscles and allows the triceps to stretch, which allows for a bigger stride. (See 'Freeing the horse's shoulder' in *Successful Schooling*, page 110).

3. Canter in a low and round frame, asking for a long, round jump in the canter. This also frees the scapula and allows triceps stretch.

4. Walk over at least six ground poles, spacing them to suit the horse. Increase the spaces gradually, but keep the first and last spaces shorter than the middle spaces. This will prevent the horse from taking an extra step between the poles and thereby shortening his stride.

5. Trot over ground poles, slowly increasing the space between each trotting pole to encourage the horse to stretch his fore and hind limbs. As with the walk exercise, the space, between the first and last trotting poles should be slightly closer, for the reasons previously explained on page 83.

6. Trot over cavalletti, increasing the height slowly. This will stretch the triceps, posterior pectoral and subscapularis muscles.

7. Put the horse in a low and round frame and push him forward to lengthen the trot. Rise higher and sit deeper while the lower leg closes around him. Ease him into the movement gradually or he will quicken his steps instead of lengthening. Start with only a few steps and not too long a stride. After about three steps do a half-halt to bring him back to collection. Push him forward again and ask for a

Trotting over ground poles. Although the distances between poles may look too great, the horse stretches to reach over them. The first and last distances are smaller, to prevent the horse from taking an extra step (see text).

Trotting over cavalletti. Note the stretch in the fetlock and anterior pectoral muscle on the leg in stance.

half-halt again. This will make him more sensitive to a light rein aid and prevent him from falling onto the forehand. Slowly build up these lengthened steps to increase the stretch. Use half- halts to prevent shortened, running steps and loss of rhythm caused by the horse falling onto his forehand. Start on a 20 m circle and once he has set up a rhythm, ride around the entire manège. This is one of the best ways to stretch the horse's leg flexors, free his shoulder and increase his stride length. You should notice a difference in a week.

8. Ride extended trot exercises. Alternate extended trot with half-halts around the entire manège. Shorten a little as you reach the corner, but ease the horse into extension again as you reach A or C. So long as you do not ride too deeply into the corners, they will help to balance the horse as he pushes for a longer extended stride. Continue around the arena a few times. You will find that the horse increases the extension with each circuit.

In addition to its other functions, counter-canter stretches the forelimb retractors. Note the stretch of the outside shoulder.

9. Counter-canter stretches the triceps, latissimus dorsi, posterior pectoral muscles, teres minor, teres major and deltoideus muscles. Start around the manège, then ride serpentines and 20 m circles. Decrease the size of the circles as the horse progresses.

10. Gymnastic jumping exercises improve the ability of the shoulder muscles to lift the horse's knees out of the way. These exercises stretch the triceps muscles. Landing after the jump stretches all the leg flexor muscles.

11. End the training session with a figure of eight of two 15–18 m circles at a lengthened trot with a fairly straight change of bend between the two circles. This is not only a good cooling down exercise, it also helps to improve the length of stride by stretching the foreleg flexors. The horse should always be stretched down to lengthen the muscles after strenuous collection exercises.

Passive Stretch Exercises for the Forelimb Retractors

Do small stretches of short duration initially and increase stretch and duration as the muscles become more flexible.

Rotations

1. These movements give only a slight stretch, as they are not held in position. They serve to promote relaxation, freer movement and loosening of the joints and are a good introduction to stretch exercises for both horse and stretcher. Rotation of the shoulder muscles and joints enables you to reach the deep muscles of the shoulder. Stand facing your horse. Remember to use the correct posture with your feet apart and your back straight. Pick the leg up then hold it with both hands above the knee. Lift the leg forwards to its point of resistance then lower it by 2 cm. The lower leg will be hanging down, with the forearm more or less parallel to the ground. Slowly rotate the forearm in complete circles. You will be drawing imaginary circles with the knee. Start with small rotations and gradually increase the diameter. Repeat a few rotations (3–5) then rotate in the other direction. Replace the foot, fully supported, to its normal position on the ground.

The first rotation exercise – drawing circles with the horse's knee.

2. Do the same rotations with the knee flexed and the cannon bone horizontal to the ground and the forearm perpendicular to the ground. Support the leg with one hand above the knee and the other holding the cannon bone. Draw imaginary circles on the ground with the knee pointing down.

3. Lift the leg and support it with one hand above the knee and the other holding the cannon bone. The forearm should be horizontal while the lower leg hangs down with the toe pointing to the ground. Draw a little circle above the ground with the point of the toe. (Slowly increase the size of the rotations during the following sessions.) Gently replace the hoof in its original position.

The second and third rotation exercises: changing the angles of the forearm and lower leg.
Note correct posture of stretcher in upper photo (see page 42 for details).

The triceps stretch.

Triceps stretch

Stand facing your horse. Slowly lift his forearm to 90° and hold it above the knee with the lower leg pointing to the ground. Stretch it forwards until resistance is felt. Hold for a few seconds, yield by relaxing, but do not let it go; stretch a little further and hold for 5–15 seconds.

Knee lift

Hold your horse's leg with both of your hands behind, but above, the knee. Slowly lift the knee straight up towards a 45° angle with the shoulder. At the first sign of resistance, lower the knee a little until the horse relaxes, then continue to lift it gently to the limb's limit. Initially it won't reach a 45° angle. Do not force the limb any further. This exercise stretches the latissimus dorsi and will help the horse to lift his limbs out of the way of the jump poles.

The knee lift.

Whole leg forward stretch

Stand facing your horse. Pick his foreleg up with one hand holding the foot and the other lightly on top of the knee. Slowly stretch the leg forwards, with the toe pointing towards your ankle. Stretch until it is straight, but do not push on the knee. Hold it in position for 5–15 seconds, and then place it back in its original position. Note the point of resistance: this is where the stretch starts. The horse may initially push his weight forwards and try to 'lean' on your hands. Release the stretch slightly and use his straight leg to push his weight backwards. When he has found his balance again you may increase the stretch. This stretches the cervical section of trapezius, latissimus dorsi, serratus ventralis cervicis, deltoideus, triceps brachii and posterior pectorals.

Forward and upward stretch

Repeat the above exercise. When the leg is straight, lift it a little to give more stretch. Hold for 5–15 seconds. As the stretch becomes easier and the horse's flexibility improves, the leg can be lifted higher, until it is almost parallel to the ground and the toe points towards your waist. This stretches the trapezius, latissimus dorsi, serratus ventralis, deltoideus and the triceps. This, and the previous exercise, also stretch the muscles associated with the carpal and digital flexor tendons and the suspensory ligament.

Once the horse can do a full leg stretch, you do not have to go through all the preliminary exercises such as the rotations and forearm stretches. Rotations should, however, be continued on horses competing at the top levels, since these rotations reach more specific muscles.

The whole leg forward stretch. Ideally, in this stretch, the knee should be straight.

The forward and upward stretch.

Stretching the Forelimb Protractors – Backward Stretch

The rearward stretches are done to keep the muscles supple and thus prevent injury.

Relevant muscles and their functions

The brachiocephalic (cleido-brachialis) muscle is the main muscle that works to pull the humerus and shoulder forwards.

Anterior superficial pectoral brings the upper arm forwards and inwards in adduction.

Supraspinatus extends the shoulder joint.

Thoracic part of trapezius tilts the top of the scapula backwards.

Biceps brachii flex the elbow and extends the shoulder joint.

Subscapularis extends the shoulder joint.

Omotransversarius helps with protraction.

Brachialis flexes the elbow joint.

Extensor carpi radialis extends the foreleg.

Thoracic part of serratus ventralis draws the top of the scapula backwards.

Deltoideus extends the shoulder joint.

Coraco-brachialis extends the shoulder.

Active Stretch Exercises for the Forelimb Protractors

All the active stretch exercises for stretching the forelimb retractors will also apply to the forelimb protractors because the further the leg stretches forwards, the further the opposite leg will move backwards. There are thus no specific active stretches for the forelimb protractors.

Passive Stretch Exercises for the Forelimb Protractors

These backward stretches are important for maintaining suppleness of the pectoral and biceps brachii muscles, which have a tendency to shorten as a consequence of their continuous use.

Start all these exercises with a small stretch, which is held for no more than 5 seconds. If the horse tolerates this, repeat and hold for 5–15 seconds.

Figure 26. The forelimb protractors to be stretched: (a) shows the superficial muscles and (b) the deep muscles.

(a)

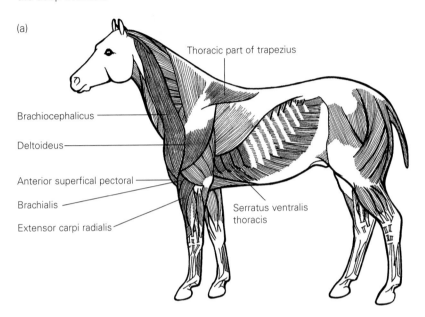

Thoracic part of trapezius

Brachiocephalicus

Deltoideus

Anterior superfical pectoral

Brachialis

Extensor carpi radialis

Serratus ventralis thoracis

(b)

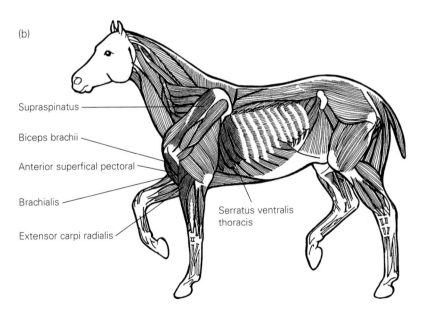

Supraspinatus

Biceps brachii

Anterior superfical pectoral

Brachialis

Extensor carpi radialis

Serratus ventralis thoracis

1. Stand next to the horse's near foreleg, facing it. Pick up the leg by pinching the superficial flexor tendon behind the cannon bone. Hold it, above the knee, with your left hand, using your right hand to support the fetlock joint. Keep the lower leg almost parallel to the ground, with the horse's knee in flexion. This gives a stronger stretch. Slowly move the horse's foreleg straight backwards towards his hind leg. Stop when the horse resists. Hold for 5–15 seconds. Rest your left elbow on your bent left knee to support your back. Slowly return the leg to its original position. This stretches the pectoral muscles, brachiocephalicus, biceps brachii, extensor carpi radialis and the thoracic section of the trapezius.

2. Once you and the horse have mastered this stretch, you can straighten the knee slowly and hold for 5–15 seconds. This stretch can be a little difficult because horses have a tendency to put their weight on the leg in an attempt to put it down.

The backward stretch, first phase.

The backward stretch, second phase.

Stretching the Forelimb Abductors – Inward Stretch

The anatomy of most of the leg joints (fore and hind) does not allow for much sideways movement. The stifle, hock, elbow, knee and fetlock joints are all hinge joints that only move in one plane, backwards and forwards. Most of the lateral movement occurs at the shoulder joint and hip joint, which are both ball and socket joints. Abduction and adduction of the foreleg is brought about by tilting the shoulder-blade outwards and inwards and by the ball and socket joint of the shoulder.

At present, the amount of detailed scientific research that has been done on stretch exercises with horses is not sufficient to answer all of our questions. For example, without proper biomechanical research, with video digitalization, it is debatable on which side (i.e. inside or outside) the relevant muscles stretch more in the lateral movements – turn on the forehand, leg-yielding, shoulder-in, travers,

115

renvers and half-pass. What is certain, however, is that the legs on either side do not stretch in the same manner. The reason for this is that the one leg will move over (or cross) in front, while the other will move behind it. Since this entails some difference in angle, it is evident that different muscles, or different parts of muscles, will stretch in each case. A second difference lies in the weight-bearing function of the legs during lateral movements. The muscles in one leg will stretch during the weight-bearing phase, while the muscles in the other leg will stretch without bearing weight. During weight-bearing, muscles have to contract to stabilize the horse. The stretch is then initiated by the muscles slowly lengthening in eccentric contraction (see Glossary). A third difference lies in the contraction-relaxation phases of the same muscles. The muscle groups of the legs on one side will alternate contraction against force with stretch at each step, when they have to 'push/pull' the horse over the leg. On the other side, the contraction will not be against this force, but will simply take the leg across without carrying the body weight. On this latter side, the antagonistic group contracts against the force of the body weight being 'pushed/pulled' over the leg.

When the horse moves laterally, the leg muscles will either pull or push the horse's body over the legs. In the first phase of the lateral movement, the horse opens his leading leg laterally and places it on the ground. In the next phase, the adductors of that leg will 'pull' the horse's body over the leg while the other leg of the pair crosses over and is placed on the ground. In the third phase, the abductors of the grounded leg will then 'push' the body over that leg while the first leg opens up laterally again and the process is repeated. Because of the underlying complexities of such movements, while it may be necessary to stretch the horse's tight side more often, it remains important that these exercises are ridden on both reins.

Relevant muscles and their functions

Supraspinatus pulls the point of the shoulder laterally and brings the leg to the outside.

Infraspinatus pulls the point of the shoulder laterally and brings the leg to the outside.

Deltoideus pulls the point of the shoulder laterally and brings the leg to the outside.

Rhomboideus pulls the scapula away from the ribcage and stabilizes the top of the scapula.

Figure 27. The forelimb abductors to be stretched: (a) shows the superficial muscles and (b) the deep muscles.

(a)

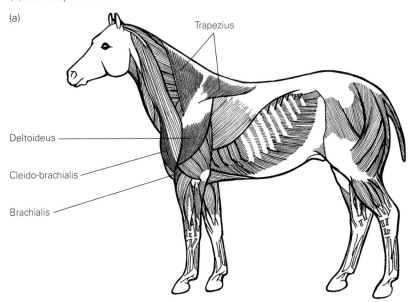

Trapezius

Deltoideus

Cleido-brachialis

Brachialis

(b)

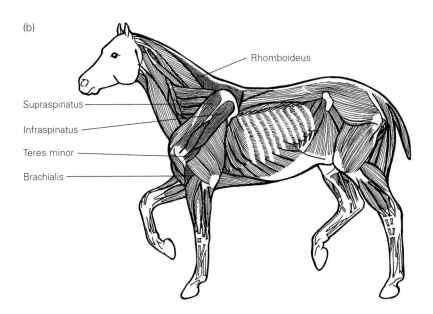

Rhomboideus

Supraspinatus

Infraspinatus

Teres minor

Brachialis

Trapezius pulls the scapula away from the ribcage and stabilizes the top of the
  scapula.
Teres minor abducts the humerus.
Brachialis abducts the humerus.
Cleido-brachialis assists abduction of the humerus.

Active Stretch Exercises for the Forelimb Abductors

By far the best way to improve lateral stretch in the horse's forelimbs is with active
stretching exercises at the walk. During lateral exercises in trot, the horse can
evade the adductor and abductor stretch by using a bigger sideways jump. The
lateral stretch exercises for stretching the forelimbs should be done in the following order of difficulty: leg-yielding; shoulder-in; travers; renvers, half-pass; pirouette.

1. Leg-yield at the walk is easier to do than half-pass, but as a result of the lack of
   bend does not give quite as much stretch as the half-pass. Therefore, start with
   leg-yield and move on to half-pass as an exercise once you and the horse have
   mastered it. The sharper the angle, the more the stretch. Increase the angle of
   the leg-yield as the horse becomes suppler, for a stronger stretch effect.

   The reasons why leg-yielding is easier to perform than half-pass are as
   follows. First, the rider uses the same (inside) leg for the bend, the push over,
   the direction and the impulsion, while the other leg remains relatively passive in
   its position behind the girth (but ready to prevent the hindquarters from leading
   the movement). This means that the movement pattern is relatively simple and
   the rider's co-ordination of aids does not have to be very advanced. Therefore,
   lateral stretch exercises in this form can be ridden at a fairly early stage of
   training. Second, the horse moves in the direction of the weight-bearing side
   and thus there is a natural impetus to assist movement in the required direction
   (to 'pull' the horse over). In half-pass, however, the rider's outside leg has to
   'push' the horse over, while the inside leg has to 'push' in a different manner and
   position, to ensure that the horse bends to the inside yet maintains his weight
   to the outside. This requires much more advanced co-ordination from the rider,
   which will naturally take time to develop. The horse also finds moving in half-
   pass bend more difficult than leg-yielding, because his weight is maintained on
   the opposite side from the direction of movement, and thus does not provide
   the same impetus as in leg-yielding.

Leg-yielding at the walk.

2. Ride shoulder-fore and shoulder-in. These exercises stretch the abductors of the inside foreleg during the crossover and, because of the inside bend, also stretch the outside leg abductors. In shoulder-in, the abductors of the inside leg stretch and contract against force alternately, thus developing strong, yet elastic muscle fibre. This exercise should be done on both reins. Start with shoulder-fore and progress to the shoulder-in. Use mainly the walk to achieve the most stretch. A shoulder-in on the circle will give a stronger stretch. Also ride shoulder-in at a sharper angle for a stronger stretch. If you want to do stretching exercises at the trot, the shoulder-in should be ridden at a medium trot for more stretch.

The shoulder-in.

Counter-canter, with the head and neck flexing away from the leading leg.

3. Counter-canter on a circle or around corners is an excellent exercise to stretch
   the abductors of the forelimb. For a stronger stretch, move the horse's head
   away from the leading leg, but ensure that he maintains the lightness of the
   forehand. If he loses lightness he will lose balance and break the canter or do a
   flying change. The reason why the horse has a tendency to do a flying change
   during the counter-canter is the result either of the righting reaction, or of
   discomfort, which leads to the stretch reflex. To avoid both these reactions the
   horse's neck must yield to the rider all the time. To ensure this, slowly bend the
   neck to the left and then slowly bend it to the right without allowing the horse
   to tighten his muscles and become hard in the hands. Start by riding around the
   arena and progress to 20 m circles, then slowly decrease the size of the circles.
   Ride a figure of eight, alternating true canter with counter-canter, the first circle
   in true canter and the second in counter-canter. Start with two 20 m circles and
   decrease the size at each attempt until you can ride two 10 m circles.

4. Ride travers, renvers and half-pass at the walk. The half-pass produces a better stretch than leg-yield for the abductors. The inside bend of the half-pass places the outside abductors in a slightly elongated frame throughout the movement. In these exercises, the abductors of the outside foreleg alternately stretch and contract against force and thus develop good quality muscle fibre. Therefore, they should be repeated on both sides. For a more progressive stretch, increase the angle and push over more. You can even do full passes. This latter is probably the best exercise to stretch the horse's legs laterally and improve on his lateral work. You will be surprised by how quickly this walk exercise will improve your lateral work.

Half-pass is a very beneficial stretch exercise.

5. Ride shoulder-in through the transitions during canter, trot, and walk. Start with shoulder-in at the walk and go directly from walk shoulder-in to trot shoulder-in and back again to walk shoulder-in. Keep alternating, but do not lose the shoulder-in. Do the same with canter shoulder-in to walk shoulder-in. This is a very difficult exercise and needs experience and time to perfect. It is nevertheless an extremely good stretch exercise.

6. Ride half- and full circle walk pirouettes. Use large as well as small circles in walk pirouette, or passade. In these exercises, the outside foreleg stretches more. The larger the circle, the greater the abductor stretch.

Passive Stretch Exercises for the Forelimb Abductors

Start with the rotation exercises, as described on pages 105–6, then progress to the proper abductor stretches.

Stand facing your horse. Lift up his near foreleg by pinching the superficial digital flexor tendon behind the cannon bone. Hold the forearm with your left hand, allowing the lower leg to hang down. Lift it to a 90° angle, but do not pull. Move his knee to the outside of your left hip. 'Hook' his foot in the space behind your knee, the sole resting against the top of your calf. By placing your legs further apart, you can extend his knee. Move your hip sideways against the horse's knee and push it to the inside. Your right hand, cupping his elbow, eases his elbow away from his ribs. This will move the distal end of the humerus away from the body. *Do not twist the horse's knee*. Hold for 5–15 seconds, then replace slowly. Aim eventually to move the one knee across the other. You can do this exercise with the horse's forearm at different heights to stretch different parts of the muscles. This stretches the posterior pectorals, triceps, supraspinatus, infraspinatus, teres minor and deltoid muscles.

This exercise can also be done with the forelimb almost straight, but with the repeated cautionary note – *do not twist the knee*. Hold the limb above the knee and at the toe. Move it over as in half-pass.

Stretching the Forelimb Adductors – Outward Stretch

The forelimb adductors should be stretched very carefully, as their primary function is to stabilize the shoulder onto the trunk. As the horse has no collar-bone (clavicle),

Forelimb abductor stretch.

these muscles have had to take over the function of the collar-bone in the human skeleton.

CAUTION: The pectoral muscles are adductors of the shoulder joint and stabilize the shoulder joint during extension (keep it against the ribcage). Therefore, full forward extension should not be performed together with abduction as this would destabilize the joint.

Relevant muscles and their functions

The anterior deep and superficial pectorals adduct and stabilize the shoulder joint during extension.

The posterior deep and superficial pectoral muscles adduct and stabilize the shoulder during extension.

Serratus ventralis stabilizes the scapula against the chest.

Coraco-brachialis adducts the forelimb.

Subclavius adducts the forelimb.

Figure 28 a–d, below and over page. The forelimb adductors to be stretched: (a) shows the superficial muscles;

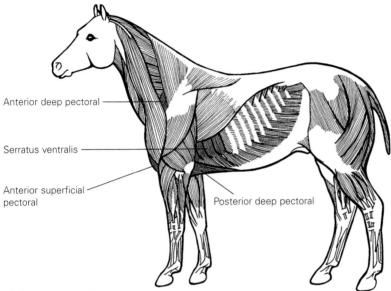

Anterior deep pectoral

Serratus ventralis

Anterior superficial
pectoral

Posterior deep pectoral

(b) the deep muscles;

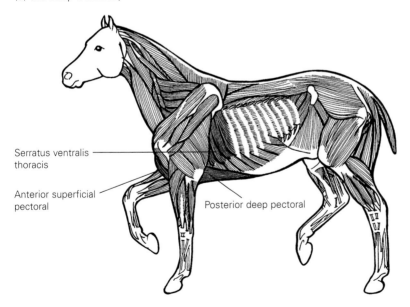

Serratus ventralis
thoracis

Anterior superficial
pectoral

Posterior deep pectoral

(c) and (d) are ventral and front views respectively.

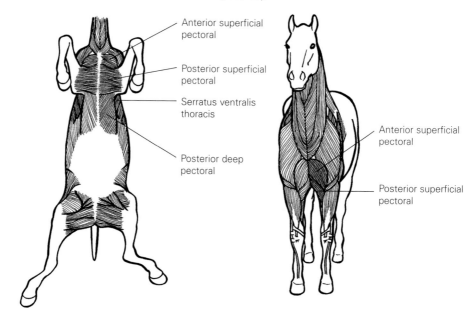

Active Stretch Exercises for the Forelimb Adductors

1. Shoulder-fore and shoulder-in at walk and at trot, as described earlier (page 120). The adductors of the outside foreleg stretch more than those of the inside leg, therefore the exercise should be done on both reins. More stretch is achieved at walk, rather than at the working or collected trot. To improve the adductor stretch at the trot, it has to be done at a lengthened gait.

2. Ride shoulder-in through all the transitions. See the exercise for abductor stretch on page 123.

3. Leg-yield at the walk, at a fairly sharp angle, is easier for horse and rider than the half-pass. Progress gradually to a sharper angle: the sharper the angle, the greater the stretch. In the leg-yield the horse places his weight on his outside (leading) shoulder. In half-pass the horse should place his weight on his outside shoulder, but often finds this more difficult than placing his weight on his inside (leading) shoulder. He then 'falls' into the half-pass and puts less stretch on the adductors. The leg-yield is thus a better stretch exercise for novices.

In addition to exercising the forelimb abductors, leg-yielding is a useful stretch exercise for the forelimb adductors.

4. Ride travers, renvers and half-pass at walk. Increase the angle and push over harder to develop more stretch. A full pass achieves the most stretch. These exercises stretch the adductors of both forelegs, but the adductors of the inside leg alternate stretch/contraction against resistance as they 'pull' the body over the leg. It is therefore important to do these exercises on both sides. If done at trot, there is less of a stretching effect.

5. Half- and full pirouettes at walk have a stretching effect on both the inside and outside foreleg adductors, but more on the inside adductor. You can do a few full pirouettes without a harmful effect. Increase the size of the circles for a stronger stretching effect.

Passive Stretch Exercises for the Forelimb Adductors

Start with the rotations described earlier (pages 105–6). Once you have mastered these rotations, you may start with the adductor stretches.

Adductor rotation stretch

Stand in front of the horse on the horse's near side, facing him. Lift up the near foreleg, allowing the lower leg to hang down. Lift the forearm to a 90° angle, but do not pull. With your left hand on the inside above the knee and your right hand flat on the elbow, push the elbow against the ribs while slowly moving the knee to the outside. Hold for 5–15 seconds. This will move the distal end of the humerus closer to the body and the shoulder joint away from the body. *This exercise should never be done with a stretched leg*, as it will have a destabilizing effect on the forelimb and knee. This exercise stretches the anterior deep and superficial pectoral muscles and the coraco-brachialis.

Adductor stretch

Stand at your horse's near side, facing him. Pick up the near foreleg with the forearm horizontal and the knee bent. Place your left arm between his leg and body, holding the elbow on the inside with your whole forearm against his forearm. Hold the cannon bone with your right hand. Stretch his forearm sideways towards your body. Do not pull on the cannon bone and avoid twisting or hyper-flexing the knee. This stretches all the forelimb adductors.

(a) Adductor rotation stretch; (b) adductor stretch.

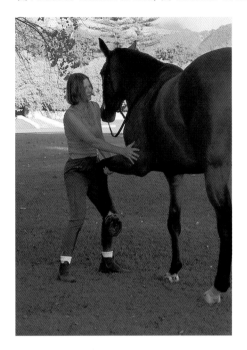 

The Hind Limbs

Stretching the hind limbs will improve engagement and the ability of the horse to use his power more effectively. It will help the horse to push for improved extended work and gives the horse the necessary equipment to improve his jumping and racing performance. The hind legs, individually, carry the entire weight of the body in the canter when only one foot is on the ground. It is therefore also important to develop equal strength in both hind limbs.

Stretching the Hind Limb Retractors – Forward Stretch

These are the power muscles of the horse that push the whole horse over his hind legs and they therefore have a major role in forward propulsion. They have to be kept very supple if they are to be effective in racing, jumping and advanced dressage.

129

Relevant muscles and their functions

Gluteus medius extends and abducts the hip.

Accessory gluteus assists the medial gluteus, but is a weak extensor.

Longissimus dorsi lumbar section extends the lumbar spine, but is connected to medial gluteus and thus assists with hip extension.

Quadratus femoris assists in hip extension.

Hamstrings:

Biceps femoris extends and abducts the hip and stifle joints.

Semimembranosus extends, adducts and rotates the hip inwards and flexes the stifle.

Semitendinosus extends the hip and flexes the stifle when not supporting weight.

Stifle flexors:

Popliteus flexes the stifle.

Gastrocnemius effects flexion of the stifle and fetlock.

Biceps femoris caudal division flexes the stifle.

Figure 29. The hind limb retractors to be stretched: (a) shows the superficial muscles and (b) the deep muscles; (c) is a rear view.

(a)

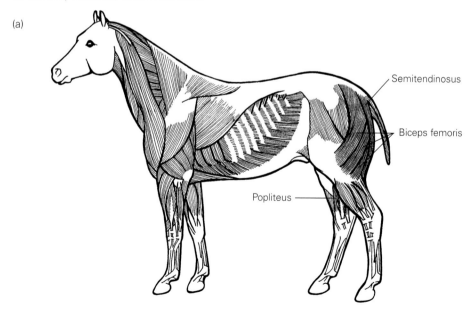

(b)

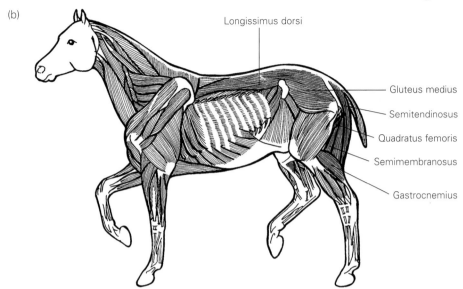

Longissimus dorsi

Gluteus medius

Semitendinosus

Quadratus femoris

Semimembranosus

Gastrocnemius

(c)

Gluteus medius

Biceps femoris

Semitendinosus

Semimembranosus

Biceps femoris

Gastrocnemius

Active Stretch Exercises for the Hind Limb Retractors

These exercises will help to improve your horse's stride length and help to prevent strain injuries of the hamstrings and gluteal muscles. A bigger movement range will help with propulsion in racing. Research has found that horses increase speed by increasing stride length, as well as by increasing stride frequency.[2] If the medial gluteal muscle is tight, the co-ordination of the stride may be lost. A major factor in the function of this muscle is to relax (do nothing) to allow the leg to plant. If the gluteals of the stance leg cannot 'switch off' at the correct time because of tightness, the swinging leg will miss the ground, swinging back and shortening the stride.

Stretching the hind leg forward will have a suppling effect on the fetlocks and will lead to a more comfortable sitting trot.

1. Riding long and low at trot and canter stretches the gluteal muscles by increasing hip flexion. It stretches the hamstrings – biceps femoris, semimembranosus and semitendinosus muscles – by extension of the stifle and flexion of the hip. Ask for a big 'jump' at the canter in this frame.

2. Ground pole exercises in both walk and trot are effective. See Active Stretch Exercises for the Forelimb Retractors, page 101.

3. Trot over cavalletti. Increase the height slowly. The horse has to flex his hind legs more, thus stretching the hip extensors.

4. Put the horse in a long and low frame and push him forward to lengthen the trot. Rise higher and sit deeper while the lower leg closes around him. Ease him into the movement gradually or he will quicken his steps. Start with only a few steps and not too long a stride. After about three steps do a half-halt to bring him back to collection. Push him forward again and ask for a half-halt again. Do this a few times, until he reacts immediately to the half-halt as well as the forward aid. This will make him more perceptive and prevent him from falling on the forehand. Slowly build up these lengthened steps to increase the stretch. Use half-halts to prevent shortened, running steps and loss of rhythm. Start on a 20 m circle and,

[2] Lindfield, B., 'Functional Anatomy of the Hind Limb of the Horse'. Lecture presented at ACPAT Spring Seminar 1998.

Ground pole work at trot. Note the stretch in the hamstrings.

once he has set up a rhythm, ride around the entire manège. This is one of the best ways to stretch the horse's hip extensors, free his shoulders and increase his stride length. You should notice a difference in a week or two.

5. Walk, trot and canter up and down hills and slopes to stretch the hamstrings and gluteal muscles. Cantering and trotting up hills stretch all the hind limb joints, lumbo-sacral, hip and fetlock joints. It increases flexion and extension of the joints through a bigger range of movement.

6. When riding out, ride your horse in a lengthened frame to stretch his muscles without the constricting influence of the dressage arena.

7. Galloping really stretches the hamstrings and gluteal muscles, but this should only be done once the horse has been stretched for some time and it is only practical for racehorses, hunters and eventers. Horses who are not fit or used to this type of work may develop a strain injury, and perhaps stress the heart and lungs.

8. Rather than galloping, ride a lengthened canter and ask for a big, slow, ground-covering 'jump'.

9. Gymnastic jumping gives a good stretch of the hamstrings and gluteal muscles as well as improving suppleness in the lumbo-sacral and hip joints – especially during the landing phase.

10. Rein-back exercises stretch the hip extensors, the stifle and hock flexors. Rein-back is not a physically easy exercise for the horse. Start with only a few steps and increase to about eight steps. You can start on a flat surface and progress to rein-back up small inclines.

Passive Stretch Exercises for the Hind Limb Retractors

All passive stretching exercises are done gently and slowly. The first effort should not be a full stretch and should only be held in position for 5 seconds. Gradually increase the stretch and duration.

Rotations

Stand at your horse's near (left) hind leg, facing backwards. Lift the leg by pinching the superficial flexor tendon behind the cannon bone. Cup the fetlock with both your hands. Lift it slightly in a forward direction and slowly draw little circles on the ground with the point of his toe, clockwise and counter-clockwise. Gradually increase the size of the circle. Sit on your haunches and rest your elbow on your bent knee to protect your back when drawing these circles. Move the leg backwards and forwards while drawing the circles.

Hamstring stretch

Stand at your horse's side, facing backwards. Pick up the hind leg by pinching the tendon behind the cannon bone (superficial flexor tendon). Should the horse put all his weight on that leg, use your shoulder to push his weight onto his other hind leg. Hold the toe with both hands either side of the hoof. Stretch the hind limb forward, in its normal movement pattern, towards the front fetlock joint, keeping the whole leg straight. Bend your knees and rest your elbow on your knee to protect your back. Stretch until you feel resistance, then relax slightly. Hold for 5–15 seconds then replace the limb in its original position. Some horses show a tendency to adduct when the hind leg is stretched forward. Should this happen, the hock may be pulled outwards to aid in abducting the leg as it is stretched forwards. The outward stretch of the hock may be done by a second person during this stretch.

Gluteal and biceps femoris stretch

Stretch the horse's leg to the fetlock as above, then slowly lift the whole leg up, pointing the foot towards the elbow joint. Initially, the horse will only be able to stretch halfway. Keep his leg as straight as possible. He will eventually be able to stretch his leg up against his abdomen.

Gastrocnemius stretch

Stretch the leg straight forwards as in the hamstring stretch (above), but put it down in a straight line with the foreleg, then pull the tail to that side to put weight on the leg. Try to stay in position next to the leg while reaching for the tail.
CAUTION: The horse may retract his leg suddenly, causing injury to himself and the handler. Be on your guard.

Stretching the Hind Limb Protractors – Backward Stretch

These muscles are powerful and play a large part in engagement of the hindquarters. The backward stretches are important to prevent the natural tendency of the hip flexors to shorten. These stretches are essential for racehorses to prevent injuries when galloping.

Relevant muscles and their functions

Sartorius flexes the hip and protracts and adducts the leg.
Tensor fascia lata flexes the hip and extends the stifle.
Gluteus superficialis flexes and abducts the hip.
Popliteus flexes the stifle.
Quadriceps femoris group:
    Rectus femoris flexes the hip and extends the stifle.
    Vastus medialis extends the stifle.
    Vastus intermedius extends the stifle.

Stretch Exercises for Your Horse

Passive stretch exercises for the hind limb retractors: (a) rotations, (b) hamstring stretch,

(a)

(b)

(c) gluteal and biceps femoris stretch, (d) gastrocnemius stretch.

(c)

(d)

Vastus lateralis extends the stifle.

Gastrocnemius flexes the stifle and extends the hock.

Long digital extensor flexes the hock.

Tibialis cranialis flexes the hock.

Lateral digital extensor flexes the hock.

Psoas major, iliacus and psoas minor form the iliopsoas muscle and run from the underside of the lumbar vertebrae and the floor of the pelvis to the femur. They flex the loin and also the hip joint, as well as drawing the hind leg forwards. The psoas minor effects lateral inclination of the pelvis.

It should be noted that the iliopsoas and quadriceps femoris play a major role in engagement of the hind leg. Working continuously in collection will put strain on them and can lead to muscle shortening. Therefore, collected work should be interspersed with riding at working and lengthened gaits.

Figure 30. The hind limb protractors to be stretched: (a) shows the superficial muscles and (b) the deep muscles; (c) is a ventral view.

(a)

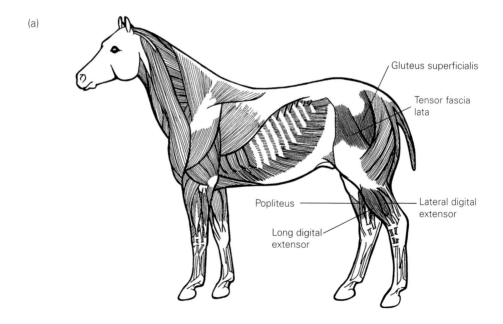

Gluteus superficialis

Tensor fascia lata

Popliteus

Long digital extensor

Lateral digital extensor

(b)

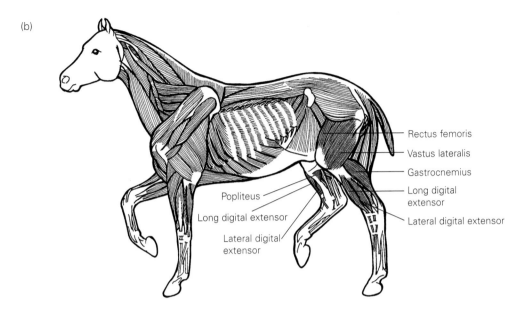

Rectus femoris

Vastus lateralis

Gastrocnemius

Long digital extensor

Lateral digital extensor

Popliteus

Long digital extensor

Lateral digital extensor

(c)

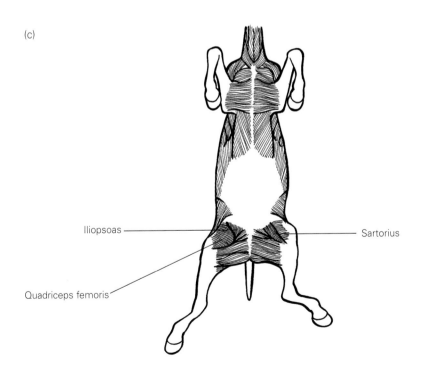

Iliopsoas

Sartorius

Quadriceps femoris

Active Stretch Exercises for the Hind Limb Protractors

All the active exercises for stretching the hind limbs forwards will apply to stretching them backwards. When the one limb stretches forwards the other will automatically stretch backwards. The further the one stretches forwards, the further the opposite leg will stretch backwards.

1. Gymnastic jumping improves suppleness in the lumbo-sacral joint as well as the hip joints. At the point of take-off, all the hip flexors are stretched.

2. Jumping exercises stretch these muscles. The higher the jump, the greater the stretch in the hind legs at the point of take-off. Heights jumped must, of course, relate to the horse's scope and level of training.

3. Gallop exercises are beneficial for the racehorse, and extended canter for other sport horses.

Passive Stretch Exercises for the Hind Limb Protractors

Start with rotations (see page 134) to loosen the joints and relax the horse. If you have already done them, you may start with the following exercises.

Rearward stretch of hip

Stand at the horse's near side, facing him. Slide your hand down his leg to warn him that you will be working on his leg. Pick up the leg by pinching the tendon (superficial flexor tendon). Hook your left arm around the front angle of his hock while your right hand supports around the fetlock. The hock should be flexed to 90°, with the tibia horizontal and the cannon bone vertical. Pull the hock slightly backwards while lifting it. This exercise stretches the quadriceps femoris, psoas major, tensor fascia lata, superficial gluteus and sartorius muscles.

Rearward stretch of hip, stifle and hock

Stand facing the horse's hind leg and pick it up as above. Hold the leg with your right hand around the cannon bone and place your left hand on top of the hock. With your right hand, gently stretch the leg backwards a little. Hold in this position, then slowly

Rearward stretch of hip.

Rearward stretch of hip, stifle and hock.

push the hock down with your left hand to straighten it. Once your horse accepts this straightening of the hock, you may stretch the whole leg backward with his foot still pointing down. Hold for 5–15 seconds. The relevant muscles (iliopsoas and quadriceps) tend to tighten easily and many horses do not seem to like having them stretched, therefore ask for this backward stretch only a little at a time. Slowly replace the leg in its original position. This stretches the iliacus, psoas major, sartorius, popliteus, tibialis cranialis and the lateral and long digital extensor muscle.

Stretching the Hind Limb Adductors

Powerful forward movement is dependent not only on the muscles that produce forward movement alone, but also on the muscles that have the dual function of forward and lateral movement, such as the biceps femoris. When observing a horse, the biceps femoris can be located on the lateral side of the hind leg. This muscle extends the hip and stifle joints, but also abducts the hind limb. In order to develop powerful protraction of the leg, this muscle has to be strengthened laterally as well as longitudinally. Therefore lateral work will enhance forward power.[3] However, in the racehorse, who traditionally does no lateral work, this area is conspicuously hollow compared to that of the dressage horse. Nevertheless, suppling the adductors while strengthening the abductors will improve forward propulsion in racing, just as it will improve upward propulsion in jumping and power in piaffe, passage and the canter pirouette. Obviously, such suppling and strengthening will also improve lateral work.

The dominant hind leg will be more difficult to abduct because the associated adductor muscles, which have to stretch, are usually stronger and shorter than their counterparts on the non-dominant leg. If the horse is 'softer' on his left rein in trot, this will be because his right side muscles are more supple. Therefore, his half-pass to the right will be easier because the weaker (right side) adductors are more flexible, so it will be easier for him to open his legs when moving to the right. Moreover, his dominant (left side) abductors have more power to push his body over his legs, towards the right.

Some horses find it difficult to spiral into a smaller circle at the canter. These horses have a tendency to adduct with the inside hind leg and cross it over the outside hind leg. This is often a consequence of weak biceps femoris, coupled with tight adductor muscles. Such horses will need to do active adductor stretches, which will often also

[3] Wegelius, Dr F., How to Maintain and Improve Athletic Performance in the Horse by Means of Passive Stretching Exercises (Lecture).

Figure 31. In this illustration the horse is left side dominant, with the left side muscles stronger, and thus less flexible. The half-pass to the right is thus easier.

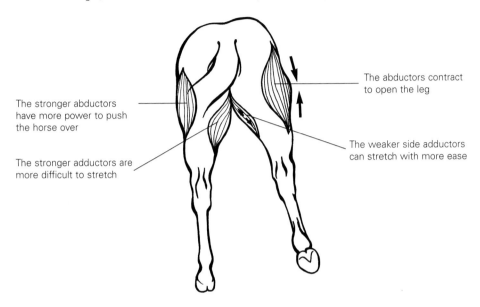

The abductors contract to open the leg

The stronger abductors have more power to push the horse over

The weaker side adductors can stretch with more ease

The stronger adductors are more difficult to stretch

help to strengthen the biceps femoris muscle. Passive adductor stretches and the hind leg hamstring stretch, combined with abduction (see Passive Stretch Exercises for the Hind Limb Retractors), will help to correct this problem.

Relevant muscles and their functions
Sartorius adducts and flexes the hip.
Gracilis adducts the hip and extends the stifle.
Adductor femoris adducts and retracts the hip.
Pectineus adducts and flexes the hip.
Semimembranosus adducts, retracts and effects inward rotation of the leg.
Semitendinosus adducts and retracts the leg.

Active Stretch Exercises for the Hind Limb Adductors
The lateral exercises used for stretching the hind limb adductors should be ridden in the following order of difficulty: turn on the forehand; leg-yield; travers; renvers; half-pass.

Figure 32. Ventral view of the hind limb adductors.

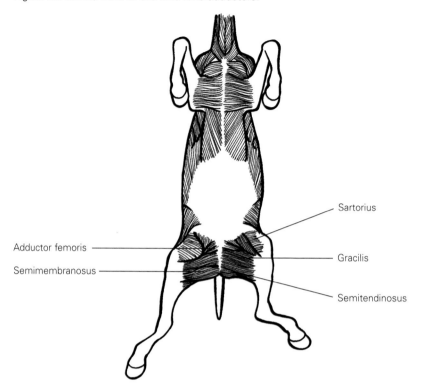

Sartorius

Adductor femoris

Gracilis

Semimembranosus

Semitendinosus

1. The turn on the forehand is the mildest stretch exercise for the hind limb adductors, but it is a good starting point and the easiest exercise for both horse and rider to perform. The horse can usually do it with greater ease to one side than the other. This is largely a consequence of the uneven development of suppleness as well as the innate weakness of the non-dominant side. Therefore, the horse will need to do more repetitions on the difficult side.

2. Leg-yielding at the walk stretches the adductors of both hind legs differently, and thus has to be done on both sides (see Active Stretch Exercises for the Forelimb Abductors).

3. Ride travers and renvers at the walk. The adductors of the leading leg alternately stretch and contract against the force of the body moving over the leg, thus

promoting better quality muscle fibre, which is strong yet elastic. These exercises should be done in both directions as the adductors of both hind legs stretch differently (see Active Stretch Exercises for the Forelimb Abductors).

4. For a more advanced stretch, ride half-pass at the walk with a sharp angle, as it has a strong stretching effect on the hind limbs. For a stronger stretch a full pass can be executed. In half-pass, the adductors of the inside leg are stretched as the leg opens and contract as it is placed on the ground and 'pulls' the body over this leg. The adductors of the outside hind leg are also stretched as the leg

Leg-yielding as an exercise for the hind limb adductors. Note the stretch of these muscles.

opens, but the subsequent contraction is not as strong because the adductors in this case only bring the outside hind leg over without the additional burden of 'pulling' the horse across. The muscles of the outside leg that do the real work are the abductors, which will 'push' the body over the leg. If the inside leg adductors are not able to stretch sufficiently, an imbalance will result in loss of rhythm ('hopping'). This comes about because the discomfort caused by the stretch reflex in the inside leg will make the horse place this leg early, and the outside leg then assists with a bigger push, thus creating the 'hopping'.

Ridden correctly, this walk half-pass makes it a really good exercise as it stretches and strengthens simultaneously. It is therefore important to do this exercise on both reins.

Passive Stretch Exercises for the Hind Limb Adductors

Rotations as described previously (page 134) are useful preparatory exercises, after which the following can be performed.

Adductor stretch

Stand at your horse's near side facing his hip. Lift the hind leg in the usual manner. Hold it with your right hand on the cannon bone or fetlock and your left arm on the inside of the stifle, supporting the stifle (and hock, if your arm is long enough). With the hock in flexion, stretch the whole leg away from the horse's body. Do not turn the toe inward or outward. Hold for 5–15 seconds. You may also hold the leg with both hands on the cannon bone to stretch it outward. This stretches the gracilis, sartorius and pectineus muscles.

Lateral-forward stretch

Lift the near (left) hind leg by the usual method. Hold the canon bone with your left hand and support the fetlock with your right hand. Rest your elbow on your knee to protect your back. Stretch the leg simultaneously forwards and sideways, keeping the hock slightly flexed. Stretch until resistance is felt, then hold for 5–15 seconds. Repeat on the other side. This stretches the adductor femoris, semimembranosus and semitendinosus muscles.

Adductor stretch (above) and lateral-forward stretch (below).

Lateral-backward stretch

Start the same way as above, but bring the leg sideways and slightly backwards to stretch different muscles at a slightly different angle. This stretches the sartorius and pectineus muscles.

Stretching the Hind Limb Abductors – Inward Stretch

When horses do active lateral movements for the first few times, or sometimes for a longer period, the stretch usually leads to discomfort in the following working trot. You will find that your horse's hind legs become bouncier after shoulder-in, leg-yield or travers. This is because of the lateral stretching of muscles that have dual functions of abduction and extension, or adduction and flexion, but which are not used to stretching laterally on a daily basis. These muscles that have dual action are:

iliopsoas – a flexor, internal rotator and adductor;
medial gluteus and deep gluteus – extensors and abductors;
superficial gluteus – flexor and abductor;
biceps femoris – extensor and abductor
semimembranosus – extensor, adductor and internal rotator.

The deep pelvic muscles are involved in joint restraint. Thus stretching can lead to some initial discomfort, the symptoms being a shortened trot with more upward push and higher steps of the hind limbs. Do not be concerned. This will happen a few times, but as soon as the horse becomes used to these lateral stretches this problem will disappear. (When you start these lateral exercises with young horses, this problem does not develop.)

Relevant muscles and their functions

Medial gluteus extends and abducts the hip joint and internally rotates it.
Deep gluteus abducts the hip joint and is a weak extensor.
Superficial gluteus flexes the hip joint and abducts the hind limb.
Biceps femoris pulls the stifle laterally outward in abduction and extends the hip and hock joint.

Figure 33. The hind limb abductors to be stretched: (a) shows the superficial muscles and
(b) the deep muscles.

(a)

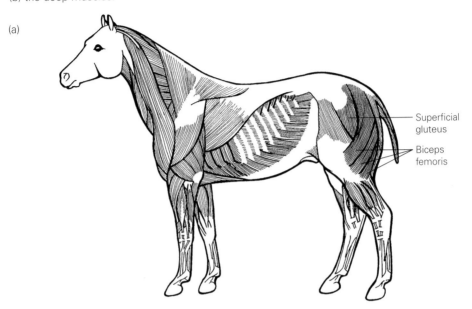

Superficial
gluteus

Biceps
femoris

(b)

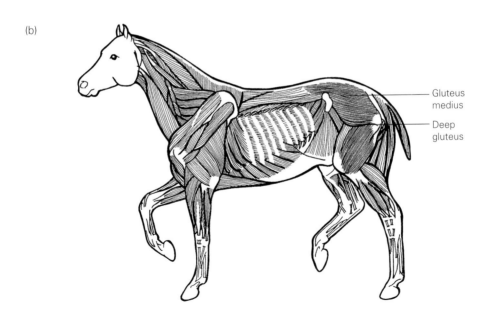

Gluteus
medius

Deep
gluteus

Active Stretch Exercises for the Hind Limb Abductors

1. The turn on the forehand is the easiest stretch exercise for the hind limb abductors. The turns should be ridden to both sides to ensure equal stretch.

2. Ride leg-yielding exercises. During leg-yielding, the inside hind leg abductors alternate stretching with contraction against force, thereby producing better quality muscle fibres. These exercises should be ridden on both reins.

3. Ride shoulder-fore and shoulder-in at walk and at medium trot, as described earlier (page 120). These exercises stretch the abductors of the inside hind leg a little, as the horse has to cross this leg over and bring it closer to the body. The exercises should thus be performed on both sides.

4. Ride shoulder-in through all the transitions (see page 123).

5. Travers and renvers at the walk stretch the abductors of both hind limbs differently. The one leg passes in front of the other, thus producing a different angle to the stretches. During travers and renvers the abductors of the outside hind stretch and contract against force alternately, 'pushing' the horse's body over his legs and developing good quality muscle fibres. These exercises should be ridden on both reins.

6. Ride half-pass at walk. In half-pass, the abductors of the outside leg are stretched and, when the horse places his foot on the ground, these same muscles contract to push the body over the leg. The abductors of the inside leg contract to open the legs and then stretch as the horse's body moves over the leg. This alternating stretching and contraction develops good quality, elastic muscle fibres. It is thus important to do this exercise on both sides. The sharper the angle, the more the stretch. The stronger the push from the rider's leg, the more the stretch.

7. Counter-canter stretches the abductors of the leading hind leg, as it has to move closer to the body around corners and during circles. This stretches the semitendinosus and biceps femoris – refer to page 121 for a more detailed description.

Half-pass at walk.

Stretch Exercises for Your Horse

Hind limb abductor stretch.

Passive Stretch Exercises for the Hind Limb Abductors

Rotations as described previously (page 134) are useful preparatory exercises, after which the following can be performed.

1. Stand beside the near side of your horse facing backwards. Pick up the off hind leg by sliding your hand down the superficial digital flexor tendon and pinching it. The horse may be a little confused, as he is not used to lifting the leg on the opposite side from the handler. If this should happen, pull his tail to the near side to place his weight on his near hind leg, then lift his off hind leg. Grasp the pastern with one hand and support the hock with the other hand. Lift it a little and bring it slowly across the other leg, pointing towards the opposite forefoot. The stifle and hock are thus moderately extended so that the hock of the stretched leg moves across in front of, and slightly above, the opposite hock. Hold the stretch for 5–15 seconds, but do not apply too much pressure as this position produces torque on the hock and stifle joints. This stretches the medial gluteus, deep gluteus and biceps femoris.

2. As the muscles become more supple, you may stretch the leg further over the other leg while keeping the hock in flexion, as in the half-pass. This stretches the medial gluteus, deep gluteus and the biceps femoris muscles.

3. The same as 2 above, but move the leg across and upwards towards your hip.

4. Stand at your horse's hindquarter on the near side. Pick the *off hind* leg up by pinching the tendon. With your right hand on the cannon bone and your left hand on his hock, keep it slightly flexed and move it backwards, down and over his near hind leg. Only carry out this stretch if you are confident that your horse will not kick. This stretches the superficial gluteus.

Conclusion

The role of horses has changed through the centuries. In this day and age their main function is to be sport horses. We have turned them into athletes for our own benefit. We therefore owe it to them to treat them accordingly. As top-class athletes they deserve to be put through a balanced training programme which does not put undue strain on their minds or bodies. This programme should develop rhythm and balance, suppleness and straightness, forward impulsion, engagement of the hindquarters and self-carriage. In order to develop these particular characteristics our horses will need strength training, fitness training and stretch exercises.

These stretch exercises, together with the strength and fitness training, should form an integral part of every equine athlete's training programme, in order to prevent strain injuries and maintain suppleness throughout the horse's career. These exercises have been developed by physical therapists during the past twenty years and are now available for all serious riders to enhance their horse's health, fitness and performance. We are indeed fortunate to have this added 'tool' to incorporate in our quest to achieve perfection in the training of the horse.

Bibliography

Belasik, P., *Dressage for the 21st Century*, J.A. Allen (London) 2002.

Budras, K.D., Sack, W.O. and Röck, S., *Anatomy of the Horse. An Illustrated Text*, Mosby-Wolfe (London) 1994.

Clayton, H.M., Training Showjumpers, in *The Athletic Horse. Principles and Practice of Equine Sports Medicine*, Hodgsen, D.R. and Rose, R.J. (eds.), W.B. Saunders Company (Philadelphia) 1994.

De la Guérinière, F.R., *School of Horsemanship* (tr. Tracy Boucher), J.A. Allen (London) 1994.

Denoix, J-M. and Paolloux, J-P., *Physical Therapy and Massage for the Horse*, Manson Publishing Ltd. (Britain) 1996.

Goody, P., *Horse Anatomy A Pictorial Approach to Equine Structure*, J.A. Allen (London) 1988.

Harris, S.E., *Horse Gaits, Balance and Movement*, Howell Book House (Macmillan Publishing Co.) (New York) 1993.

Hodges, J., Supporting the Dressage Horse with Sport Science (Art.), *Dressage* August 1999.

Hodgson, D.R. and Rose, R. J., *The Athletic Horse. Principles and Practice of Equine Sports Medicine*, W.B. Saunders Company (Philadelphia) 1994.

Hourdebaigt, J-P., *Equine Massage*, Howell Book House (A Simen & Schuster Macmillan Company) (New York) 1997.

Jones, W. E., *Equine Sportsmedicine*, Lea & Febiger (Philadelphia) 1989.

Kaselle, M. and Hannay, P., *Touching Horses – Communication, Health and Healing through Shiatsu*, J.A. Allen (London) 1995.

Kautto, M., Stretching of the Horse (Poster), Alingsås (Sweden).

Lockhart, R.D., Hamilton, G.F. and Fyfe, F.W., *Anatomy of the Human Body*, Faber and Faber Ltd. (London) 1965.

Meagher, J., *Beating Muscle Injury for Horses*, Hamilton Horse Associates (Hamilton, Massachusetts) 1985.

Möller, M., Oeberg, B., Ekstrand, J. and Gillquist J., The Effect of a Strength Training Programme on Flexibility (Art.), Swedish Society of Sports Medicine 1981.

Nelson, H., *François Baucher the Man and his Method*, J.A. Allen (London) 1992.

Porter, M., *The New Equine Sports Therapy*, The Blood-Horse, Inc. (Lexington) 1998.

Rossi, E.L. and Check, D., *Mind-Body Therapy, (Psycho-biology of Injury and Physiological Tissue Memory)*, W. Norton & Co. (USA) 1994.

Smythe, R.H. and Goody, P.C., *The Horse Structure and Movement*, J.A. Allen (London) 1998.

Snow, Dr D.H. and Vogel, C.J., *Equine Fitness. The Care and Training of the Athletic Horse*, Trafalgar Square Farm Book, David and Charles, Inc. (North Pomfret) 1987.

Spencer, N., The Barn Companion (Poster), Equitonics, Fairfax Station (Virginia).

Spring, H., Illi, U., Kunz, H., Röthlin, K., Schneider, W. and Tritschler, T., *Stretching and Strengthening Exercises*, Thieme Medical Publishers, Inc. (New York) 1991.

Travell, J.G., MD, Simons, D.G., MD, *Myofascial Pain and Dysfunction –The Trigger Point Manual*, Williams and Wilkens (Los Angeles) 1983.

Wyche, S., The Balance of Change. Tissue Transformations – As if by Magic? (Art.) *Dressage* August 2000.

Zidonis, N. and Soderberg, M. K., *Equine Acupressure. A Treatment Workbook. A Hands-on Approach to Your Horse's Well-being*, Equine Acupressure, Inc., (Printed by Parker Printing Inc.) (Colorado) 1991.

Index

Index

Index